Get Wise!™
MASTERING
Writing
SKILLS

**Laurie Sue Barnett
& Heather McCarron**

THOMSON
━✦━
PETERSON'S

Australia • Canada • Mexico • Singapore • Spain • United Kingdom • United States

THOMSON
PETERSON'S

About Thomson Peterson's

Thomson Peterson's (www.petersons.com) is a leading provider of education information and advice, with books and online resources focusing on education search, test preparation, and financial aid. Its Web site offers searchable databases and interactive tools for contacting educational institutions, online practice tests and instruction, and planning tools for securing financial aid. Thomson Peterson's serves 110 million education consumers annually.

For more information, contact Thomson Peterson's, 2000 Lenox Drive, Lawrenceville, NJ 08648; 800-338-3282; or find us on the World Wide Web at www.petersons.com/about.

Man, this page is boring!

Get Wise! Mastering Writing Skills   0-7689-1078-1

Printed in Canada
10 9 8 7 6 5 4   04

Acknowledgments

A special thanks to my co-author, Heather McCarron. This book would not have been complete without your alien essay! Thanks to Mandie Rosenberg for drawing the original sketch of Chi; Gary Van Dzura for the professional rendering of Chi and making her come to life; Greg Wutke for his great book design; Ilene Colletti, for her annoying (but wise!) comments; and Alex Colletti for his sage advice on the "Chi bars."

There were many others involved in the creation of Chi and *Get Wise!* But I would like to particularly thank: Bernadette Webster, Michele Able, Wallie Hammond, Lori Frescas, and Farah Pedley. Thanks to Eric Goldwyn for his encouragement and irreverent humor (he forced me to say that!).

Finally, thanks to Brian Phair for his unending support and love, and sorry for all the lost weekends (although you did get to watch all those games!).

—Laurie Barnett

There are a ton of people who I ought to thank, but a handful really stand out:

All of my teachers, especially Dorothy Zimms, Harry Schultz, and Ilona McGuiness.

Everyone whose brains I picked, including Alysha Bullock, Mike Carvin, Craig Heinz, Megan Hellerman, Melissa Masi, and Céline Rey-Bellet.

My fellow writer, Laurie Barnett, for putting up with all of my drafts (yes, Reader, even writers have trouble writing sometimes!)

And Mom and Dad, for making all of those tuition payments.

—Heather McCarron

Contents

1. Have extraterrestrials visited earth?

2. Do today's teen pop stars have any musical talent?
(An Argument Essay)

3. Should pep rallies be an integral part of the high school experience?
(An Argument Essay)

4. Who makes a better pet, a cat or a dog? (A Compare/Contrast Essay)

5. If you could pick three people to live with in "The Real World"
house, who would you pick and why?

6. Defend or refute the following statement from the film
Forrest Gump: "Life Is Like a Box of Chocolates—You Never Know
What You're Going to Get."

7. Write an essay in which you compare or contrast the heroes from
your two most-favorite action/adventure films.

introduction

You've got your pen in hand, ready to create what you hope will be a work of genius. A lot is riding on what you're about to write, and the pressure is overwhelming. But nothing happens. You have no idea how to even *start*. The paper just stares back at you, blank and vacant. You throw down your pen and scream for help.

Oh, come on! Writing is a piece of cake! You want to express joy? Just stick a smiley face or LOL at the end of your sentence. You want depression? Sadness? Pathos? A :(or {:{ will do the trick!

1

www.petersons.com   *Get Wise! Mastering Writing Skills*

Sorry, Chi, but e-mail shortcuts and emoticons won't fly with your teachers. The world of e-mail encourages this strange, abbreviated style of communication, but nine times out of ten, this kind of writing leads to a misunderstanding. You might have written something funny, but your reader could be insulted if he or she doesn't see the :) at the end of your message. The easiest way to avoid miscommunication—or no communication at all—is to write well-constructed and easily understood prose.

And that's why you've opened this book. We've been there, done that, bought the T-shirt and more in our quest to conquer the Mount Everest known as writing. We know what it takes to impress teachers. And you will, too, once you've finished this book.

You may know a lot more about writing than you think. We'll prove it to you with the following quiz:

1. Of the following, who is a writer?
    (A) Chewbacca the Wookie
    (B) Kermit the Frog
    (C) Ghengis Khan
    (D) The Old Woman Who Lived in a Shoe
    (E) Dave Barry

    The correct choice is (E). Even if you've never heard of Dave Barry, we're hoping you were able to figure out that the others definitely *weren't* writers!

2. In the following sentence, which word is a noun?

The green frog jumped high.
(A) the
(B) green
(C) frog
(D) jumped
(E) high

The correct choice is ... yes, (C). We really hope you didn't get this one wrong. It isn't the purpose of this book to teach you grammar, so if you did get it wrong, check out another Peterson's title, *Get Wise! Mastering Grammar Skills.* You'll learn all about the parts of speech, as well as a bunch of other grammar-related stuff.

Now try this question:

3. An essay is _____.
(A) longer than a sentence, shorter than a book.
(B) factual.
(C) a way in which a writer can express himself.
(D) informative.
(E) all of the above.

The correct choice is (E). Now you can see that you already know something about writing. So to see whether you've got what it takes to become a *good* writer, here's one last question:

4. Which of the following best describes your approach to writing?

   (A) *I daydream.* It doesn't take much to send my eyes wandering off the paper and into outer space.

   (B) *I panic.* The mere mention of a writing assignment makes me break out in a sweat, hyperventilate, and feel like my lunch is going to come right up out of my stomach.

   (C) *I procrastinate.* I put it off until the day before an assignment's due, and then I stay up all night, trying to work a miracle as the minutes tick by on my watch.

   (D) *I'm a perfectionist.* I'll spend an hour writing and rewriting the same sentence until it's absolutely right.

   (E) *I don't squirm, I don't put it off, and I don't nit-pick over every detail.* I just sit down, write a pretty good essay, and get a decent grade.

The correct choice is (E), or at least it *will* be by the time you finish this book. Don't believe us? Well, no matter what you may think, we believe you *DO* have what it takes. We'll let you in on a secret: There is a formula to writing a good essay, and it *is* within your reach because we're going to give you that formula— and more. But we won't lie to you either. No fairy godmother is going to tap you on the head with her magic wand and give you the ability to write well. It's going to take some work as well as some determination, but, as in anything else in life, the more you practice, the better you'll get and the easier it'll be. Even Stephen King, Charles Dickens, and J. K. Rowling had to practice before they became masters of prose!

So pick your pen back up and let's get started!

chapter 1

Words That Stick

(or How to Make Word Magnets)

If there were no gravity, the Earth would fly away from the sun and hurl endlessly into deep space. Life as we know it would cease to exist.

Science? Uh oh! Or is this a metaphor? Hope I don't have the wrong book!

5

Get Wise! Mastering Writing Skills   *www.petersons.com*

OK, Chi. Stay with us. Unlike the natural invisible glue (which we call gravity) holding our planet to the sun, words are funny things. For the most part, a word simply sitting by itself on a piece of paper will fly apart and have no meaning at all. Check this out:

The

The *what?* And what did the *what* that is not actually there *do? Duh!* We all know that most words need other words before or after them in order to *mean* something.

OK then. You're probably right, Chi. How's this?

Dog? the ate

Here's my question: Who needs this book, us or *you?* We know you have to put words into some kind of *order* for them to make sense.

Thanks, Chi. Exactly our point. In order for words to "stick" together and make sense, they need us! Words need to be *arranged* in specific ways in order to *say* anything.

Also, things like punctuation need to be correct *and* placed correctly. Although we make an obvious example here, the point is that words need something from us in order to stick together and have meaning to a reader. So, let's try it again:

The dog ate.

The words are in the right order now. We have replaced the question mark with a period and placed it on the end of what now is a sentence. But something's still wrong, isn't it? While the words make sense, we are left with a lot of questions. What did the dog eat? How did the dog eat it? What kind of dog was it?

And, most of all, who cares?

That's why we need more words with stronger glue to make better sense. And to make your reader, or Chi, care, we need something more than the ability to put words in the right order and insert punctuation—although that's a good start! Check this out instead!

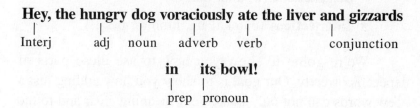

Hey, the hungry dog voraciously ate the liver and gizzards
Interj   adj   noun   adverb   verb   conjunction

in its bowl!
prep pronoun

Well, now we're saying something!

Yeah, you are saying something, and it is pretty weird. May I please go now?

OK, we know that's a pretty silly sentence, but it *is* something: It's silly *and* weird! So, the glue we need to make our words stick and talk to the reader is basically the eight parts of speech!

EIGHT STICKY PARTS OF SPEECH

* ★ **Nouns** (aardvark, Brillo, Chi, never-neverland)

* ★ **Verbs** (sang, pooped, forgot, slept)

* ★ **Pronouns** (he, she, us, them)

* ★ **Adjectives** (crazy, yucky, mucky, cool)

* ★ **Adverbs** (boldly, quite, delightfully)

* ★ **Prepositions** (into, through, under, over)

* ★ **Conjunctions** (if, and, but, or)

* ★ **Interjections** (eureka! uh, hmmm, pssst!)

We're going to show you how to use these parts of speech correctly. Our goal is to show you how adding just a few words can not only make your meaning clear and to the point but also liven up your thoughts. The first exercise in this book will get your pen warmed up and (hopefully) be a mildly entertaining way to get you thinking about how much of an impact a few carefully chosen words can have.

Get Wise!

Have you ever played Mad Libs™? You know, those fill-in-the-blank games where you end up with some wacky sentences? On a separate sheet of paper, write down any examples of the following parts of speech. Don't peek at the paragraph on the next page until you're done!

1. **PREPOSITION**

2. **ADVERB**

3. **NOUN**

4. **NOUN**

5. **VERB**

6. **NOUN**

7. **VERB** (past tense)

8. **ADJECTIVE**

9. **ADVERB**

10. **NOUN**

Now insert your words into this passage:

Once _____ a time, in a land far, far
         PREPOSITION

_____ there lived a young _____ named
ADVERB   NOUN

Cinderella. Every day, Cinderella had to iron the

_____ , _____ the house, and cook the
    NOUN   VERB

_____ while her evil stepmother and stepsisters
    NOUN

_____ in the garden. Until she met the
    VERB

_____ prince, Cinderella believed she would
ADJECTIVE

_____ be the family's _____ .
   ADVERB   NOUN

Here's what Chi ended up with:

Once **INTO** a time, in a land far, far **CRANKY**, there
lived a young **GIRAFFE** named Cinderella. Every day,
Cinderella had to iron the **POCKETBOOK**, **TRAMPLE** the
house, and cook the **FROGS** while her evil stepmother and
stepsisters **SAILED** in the garden. Until she met the **PESKY**
prince, Cinderella believed she would **CRANKILY** be the
family's **CACTUS**.

You can come up with some pretty weird pieces by just
throwing some parts of speech into the mix. The point is that
by picking the *right* words you can say exactly what you
want, and perhaps in intriguing and lively ways.

GET STICKY (OR *SPECIFIC*)

Take a look at the following sentence:

There is a tree in my backyard.

Now describe that tree. Can't do it, can you? Or maybe you guess that it's a flowering magnolia or a maple sapling, but unless our sentence is more specific, you'll have to go out on a limb (no pun intended!) and make something up. Maybe it'll help if we say,

There is a weeping willow in my backyard.

That narrows it down and makes a huge difference! A word like *tree* can be interpreted to mean any of several hundred species of trees, but with the English language, you've got a collection of tools that will let you get specific and nail down exactly what you're trying to say.

Webster's New Third International Dictionary contains more than 450,000 words, starting at *aardvark* and going straight through to *zyzzogeton*. Chances are you don't know all of the words that appear in between—and no one expects you to! But keeping a good dictionary and thesaurus by your side will help you replace *stale* and *vague* words with alternatives that will make your writing *interesting* and *informative*. Take a look at the following sentence with nonspecific words:

Dishes covered with food were in the sink.

Just like the earlier *tree* example, the nonspecific words in this sentence force the reader to fill in missing details, and unless the reader has seen the sink for himself, there's a strong possibility that he'll fill in the wrong details. However, if we replace the nonspecific words with specific ones, we won't have to worry about the reader not getting the right picture:

> ## Plates and glasses encrusted with spaghetti sauce and milk were piled in the sink.

The reader knows what kind of dishes were in the sink (*plates* and *glasses*), what kind of food was on them (*spaghetti sauce* and *milk*), the approximate age of the food (*encrusted* means it's been sitting out in the open for a while), and the amount of dishes in the sink (*piled* evokes an image of a stack of dishes). Now there aren't any doubts in the reader's mind because we got specific with our words.

Of course, too much of a good thing can backfire. Picking the fanciest, biggest, most impressive-sounding word won't win any points with your teacher—especially if the word is so obscure and unusual that now *she* has to go to the dictionary or thesaurus to figure out what it means! So make sure your words sound like something you'd actually say, as well as something your reader will be familiar with.

Here's a sentence riddled with specific words that aren't likely to be part of your everyday vocabulary:

> ## I execrate my irksome fraternal sibling because lately I have espied that he enjoys beleaguering and abasing me in front of my intimates.

Your reader will probably give up reading your sentence by the third time he's visited the dictionary. The following might be easier for most readers to digest:

> I hate my annoying brother because lately I have noticed that he enjoys teasing and humiliating me in front of my friends.

Or as Chi likes to say:

My brother is a butthead.

Get Wise!

In the following sentences, replace the underlined nonspecific words with specific words you would use in everyday conversation. Keep your thesaurus and dictionary at your side to help you while you work and use them often.

1. That <u>business</u> sells <u>goods</u>.

2. The <u>woman</u> <u>listens</u> to <u>music</u>.

3. The <u>animal</u> <u>crossed</u> the <u>road</u>.

4. She <u>dropped</u> <u>liquid</u> on the <u>equipment</u>.

5. The <u>bird</u> flew out of the <u>tree</u>.

How Wise?

Sentences will vary. These are examples.

1. That <u>toy store</u> sells <u>Silly Putty</u>.

2. My <u>grandmother</u> <u>grooves</u> to <u>reggae</u>.

3. <u>The computer-animated frog</u> <u>hopped</u> across the <u>twelve-lane digital highway</u>.

4. She <u>spilled</u> <u>pink</u> <u>hair dye</u> on the <u>computer</u> <u>keyboard</u>.

5. That <u>rose-breasted</u> <u>cockatoo</u> flew out of the <u>maple tree</u>.

APPROPRIATE WORDS

There's more to writing than just picking specific words from the thesaurus and dictionary. The words have to make sense in the *context* of your sentence. Take a look at the following sentences:

A thief *ransacked* Grandma's attic for valuables.

Grandma *ransacked* her attic for her old photo album.

Ransacking usually refers to robbery. While it makes sense for a thief to ransack Grandma's attic, it doesn't make a lot of sense for Grandma to ransack her own attic because she can't steal from herself. Instead, it makes more sense for

Grandma to *rummage through* or *search* her attic for the photo album. So that means you need to *think* about your words before you put them on paper.

Further, you need to choose words that are appropriate for your *audience*. For example, if you're writing something that is scientific or technical, like a lab report for biology class, your teacher may expect you to use the phrase *homo sapiens*. But if this were for a history class, your teacher may react oddly. Instead, your history teacher would probably be happier if you used the more familiar and less technical *man*, just as your English teacher probably wouldn't mind seeing *dude* in your short story about surfers. Again, choosing the right words has everything to do with *who* is reading. Words like *undead*, *bloodsucker*, and *crypt* might make more sense to someone who reads Anne Rice's vampire novels while *pow* and *blam* work only for *Batman* comics.

So it's okay to tell your *mommy* you have a *boo-boo* when you're 3 years old. But when you're 14, you'll tell your *mom* that you've got a *cut*. Then your doctor will tell your *mother* that he's going to suture your *laceration*.

Get Wise!

Replace each of the following words in parentheses with something that is more appropriate. Again, feel free to use your dictionary or thesaurus for help.

1. The aggressive rottweiler (yapped) at the letter carrier.

2. My 2-year-old brother (imputes) me when he scribbles on the walls.

3. Every time Aunt Mabel sees me, she says she can't believe how much I've (expanded).

4. Water (congeals) when the temperature drops below 32 degrees.

5. An orange is surrounded by an (integument).

6. Popular young (personages) like Justin Timberlake and Christina Aguilera are called teen (luminaries).

7. My parents have each other's name (chiseled) on the inside of their wedding bands.

8. When I was a kid, my family spent all of our summer vacations at the (littoral).

9. Breaking a mirror causes (infelicity) for seven years.

10. Before you can plant a tree, you must (excavate) a (cavity) in the ground.

How Wise?

It's okay if your answers are not the same as ours.
There is often more than one appropriate word to replace nonspecific words.

1. The aggressive rottweiler <u>growled</u> at the letter carrier.

2. My 2-year-old brother <u>blames</u> me when he scribbles on the walls.

3. Every time Aunt Mabel sees me, she says she can't believe how much I've <u>grown</u>.

4. Water <u>freezes</u> when the temperature drops below 32 degrees.

5. An orange is surrounded by a <u>rind</u>.

6. Popular young <u>stars</u> like Justin Timberlake and Christina Aguilera are called teen <u>idols</u>.

7. My parents have each other's name <u>engraved</u> on the inside of their wedding bands.

8. When I was a kid, my family spent all of our summer vacations at the <u>seashore</u>.

9. Breaking a mirror causes <u>bad luck</u> for seven years.

10. Before you can plant a tree, you must <u>dig</u> a <u>hole</u> in the ground.

ACTIVE VOICE (OR HOW TO MAKE YOUR NOUNS *MOVE*)

We've learned how to make words "stick" together and have meaning in a sentence, but how do you make these words *interesting?* The difference between the *active* and *passive* voice can make all the difference in your writing. While using the passive voice is not necessarily incorrect, it is usually boring! Nothing will send your reader off to La-La Land faster than sentences written in the passive voice because they'll zap the energy right out of your writing. Take a look at this:

The cheating student was caught by the teacher.

What's wrong with this sentence? The subject, *the cheating student*, doesn't actually *do* anything. Instead, the action is performed by the object, *the teacher*, which makes the sentence passive. Let's look at this again:

The cheating student was caught by the teacher.
(subject)   *(verb phrase)*   *(acting noun)*

The above sentence, as well as just about every passive sentence, contains these two problems:

- ★ The first word in the verb phrase includes the word *is, am, are, was, were, be, been,* or *being*

- ★ The acting noun (in this case, *the teacher*) is at the <u>end</u> of the sentence and introduced with the word *by*

So here's our trick for instantly transforming a boring *passive* sentence into a more interesting, *active* sentence:

★ Move the *acting noun* up to the *front* of your sentence.

Watch what happens:

The teacher caught the cheating student.
(acting noun) *(verb)*   *(subject)*

Although the meaning is essentially the same, the sentence *sounds* different. There is an instant picture in the reader's mind because you don't need to think about the sentence in order to get its meaning. An added bonus to using active verbs: The active version uses fewer words. Go ahead. Count them. The active sentence is less wordy than the passive, which is always a good thing, even if it's only a two-word difference. If you can convey your meaning with fewer words, your reader will have an easier (and faster) time getting what you've written.

Is it ever okay to be passive?

I use the passive voice every night at dinner. After we finish eating I sit *passively* at the dining table and say I have a stomach ache so my brother has to clear the dishes! Then I patiently watch everyone else clean up! Works like a charm!

Sure, Chi, and we bet you could think of a lot more reasons to be passive. But what about in writing? It is okay to use the passive voice when you don't know who performed the action. For instance:

My wallet was stolen.

An anonymous tip was left on the police station's answering machine.

The phrase "by someone unknown" is implied in both of these sentences. And since you don't know who's the acting noun, you can't move that unknown to the beginning of the sentence!

Get Wise!

Try making the following sentences active:

1. The song was performed by the aging British rock stars.

2. The skateboard will be ridden by Bart.

3. Malcolm is being chased by his brother Reese.

4. The funky chicken dance was performed by the wedding guests.

5. A tennis racket was thrown at the referee by the temperamental athlete.

How Wise?

1. The aging British rock stars performed the song.

2. Bart will ride the skateboard.

3. Reese chased his brother Malcolm.

4. The wedding guests performed the funky chicken dance.

5. The tempermental athlete threw his tennis racket at the referee.

DESCRIPTIVE WORDS

Take a look at this sentence:

The waitress placed the dessert on the table.

While there's nothing grammatically wrong here, the words just kind of sit there on the page. Do you care about this waitress? No. So why read on? Something has to pull you in and get you interested. Here's where word magnets come in. Why do we call descriptive words *word magnets*? Have you ever held up two magnets and felt the energy between them? Adjectives, or descriptive words, create a kind of energy. Let's try adding a few descriptive details to the words above and see what happens:

The agitated waitress placed the melting ice cream sundae on the wobbly table.

A few details not only create a more complete picture of the waitress and the state of the table but also they bring the reader closer to the world the writer is creating. The waitress is *agitated*, the ice cream is *melting*, and the table is *wobbly*. Get the sense that something may *happen*? Now you've got a *reason* to read on and see. Again, a few words and a couple of details make all the difference between a flat, static scene and a live, bustling world where things melt and people get upset.

Purple Prose

Believe it or not, though, there's a drawback to being *too* descriptive. In the world of writing, there is something called *purple prose*. What's that? It means adding words for the sake of filling up your paper with lots of unnecessary information. You'll end up with "purple prose" that attracts attention to itself and takes the attention away from what you're actually trying to say! What if you overdescribed that sentence about the waitress and the sundae?

Maria, an agitated seventeen-year-old high school student working after school as a waitress, wore a red T-shirt and a pair of flare-leg jeans and had a fringe of wispy bangs above her pale blue eyes as she placed the hot fudge and chocolate ice cream sundae that was melting so that its whipped cream oozed over the sides of the glass and on to the wobbly table that was spread with a red-and-white checked, vinyl tablecloth.

Phew! By the time you get to the period at the end of the sentence, you have no idea what the whole thing is supposed to be about because there is *so* much description. Who cares what Maria's wearing, or that she has blue eyes, or that there's a red-and-white checked, vinyl tablecloth on the table? All of that detail detracts from the purpose of the original sentence: to set up a scene in which the waitress is agitated.

REDUNDANCIES

You must first and foremost be able and willing to eliminate each and every redundant and repeated phrase in your writing.

What's redundant? For starters, any phrase that unnecessarily repeats similar words, like "first and foremost," "able and willing," "each and every," and "redundant and repeated." These phrases have become so much a part of our everyday language that most of us don't even realize we use them.

Here are a couple of Chi's favorites:

advance warning

Duh! Don't warnings always come in advance?

audible sound

What else can a sound be? Visual?

close proximity

Uh, I think if something's close, it may already be in proximity!

end result

Last time I checked, results always come at the end!

exact replica

Aren't replicas always exact?

final outcome

Outcomes are pretty much final.

free gift

The very nature of a gift is that it's free. Unless, of course, it's from my brother, and then there's always some ulterior motive lying behind it!

in my own personal opinion

Whose opinion would I be writing about if not my own? Unless, of course, I'm writing with one of my other personalities!

past history

Doesn't all history occur in the past?

true facts

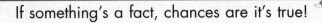

If something's a fact, chances are it's true!

Or, as Homer Simpson would say: "Facts are meaningless. They can be used to prove anything even remotely true."

An easy trick for keeping redundancies out of your writing is to avoid using the following words:

very

totally

utterly

completely

majorly (Is that a word?)

Sure, they're descriptive, but they're almost always useless. For example, you can't get more exhausted than exhausted, so *totally* exhausted is, you've got it, REDUNDANT!

CLICHÉS

Clichés are expressions that, once upon a time, were unique and creative. But they've been used so much over the years that now they're dull and worn out. Think of a cliché as though it were a song that you really loved when it first came out three months ago, but lately you've been hearing it everywhere—on the radio and in videos, in movie soundtracks and commercials, even at high school marching band performances. And now you're sick and tired of it.

Teachers feel the same way about clichés. They've read them so many times over the years that all they'll want to do is scream when they see them in your essay. If you find that a colorful phrase has flowed smoothly from your pen, take a second look at it. You've probably used a cliché.

Here are a few of the most popular has-been phrases:

ballpark estimate

big as a whale

black as night

bored to tears

can't see the forest from the trees

clear as a bell

free as a bird

happy as a clam

hungry like a wolf

leave no stone unturned

needle in a haystack

quick as a rabbit

straight from the heart

sweet as sugar

young at heart

VERBAL TICS

Last—and certainly least—are verbal tics. There are some words that you just can't help but use all the time. When you talk to a friend, you might insert "like" every time you need to take a breath. Or when you walk away from an argument, you might replace an expletive with the less offensive but still snotty-sounding "whatever." Believe it or not, the same thing happens in writing, and usually the offending words are transitions such as:

then

like

so

though

anyway

It is fine to use these once in your writing, but many writers latch on to a single transition, which they use *every* time they connect sentences to one another. For example, let's say your personal tic is the transition *then*:

My brother and I got into a huge fight last night. I was watching "The Simpsons" in the living room, but <u>then</u> he walked in and changed the channel to "The Sopranos" without asking me if I minded. So <u>then</u> I yelled at him, and <u>then</u> he smacked me across the back of the head. <u>Then</u> I pinched his arm really hard, and <u>then</u> he bit my wrist. <u>Then</u> I pounded his leg with my fist, and <u>then</u> he kicked me in the knee. <u>Then</u> Mom came into the room and screamed at us. <u>Then</u> we were grounded for a month, and now neither one of us can watch any TV.

Sounds repetitive, huh? Maybe even a little childish? With a little forethought and creativity, you can avoid this problem. If you find that you unintentionally repeat the same word throughout your essay, go to the thesaurus to find an alternative.

Here are two more Mad Libs™ for you to try. But this time, you'll be changing some famous words:

1. **VERB**

2. **PREPOSITION**

3. **NOUN**

4. **NOUN**

5. **NOUN**

6. **VERB**

_____ _____ little star
VERB   REPEAT VERB 1

How I wonder what you are

Up _____ the _____ so high
PREPOSITION   NOUN

Like a _____ in the sky.
NOUN

Twinkle twinkle little _____
NOUN

How I _____ what you are.
VERB

Here's Chi's version:

HEAVE HEAVE little star

How I wonder what you are

Up UNDER the LIZARD so high

Like a JELL-O in the sky.

Twinkle twinkle little SHARK

How I HICCUP what you are.

It just doesn't have the same effect as the original, huh? Well, since this exercise is so much fun, let's try it again:

1. **VERB**

2. **NOUN**

3. **ADJECTIVE**

4. **NOUN**

5. **VERB ENDING IN -ING**

All right, hold on to your hat, because you're about to change one of Shakespeare's most famous plays:

To _____ or not to _____ ,
VERB   REPEAT VERB 1

that is the question:

Whether 'tis nobler in the _____ to suffer
NOUN

The slings and arrows of _____ fortune
ADJECTIVE

Or to take arms against a _____ of troubles,
NOUN

And by _____ end them.
VERB ENDING IN -ING

Here's what Chi ended up with:

To **BARK** or not to **BARK**, that is the question:

Whether 'tis nobler in the **MONKEY** to suffer

The slings and arrows of **ORANGE** fortune

Or to take arms against a **CUPCAKE** of troubles,

And by **GALLOPING** end them.

Simply paying a little attention to your words will go a long way to impressing a "professional" reader like a teacher. The next step is putting the words together. So, onward and upward, let's go to Chapter 2!

chapter 2

Sentences That
Zig and Zag
(or How to Make Your Words Move!)

Like words, sentences can also fall into the habit of sitting
lifelessly on a page with nothing to do or say. We just learned
how to put words together so that they have energy and zip.
Now we need to look at stringing our words together into
sentences that express more complicated thoughts. In Chapter 1, we learned that words need to be used correctly in order
to best convey your thoughts to a reader. Sentences will need
your direction as well. In fact, this is where real writing begins! By "real writing," we mean more than just stating facts
or opinions. It's *how* you state your facts and opinions. And
there is more than one correct way to write about something;

actually there are lots of ways to write about something, and they may all be correct. But not all of them will have *style*.

Think of it like this. We *all* wear T-shirts. But the way *I* wear *my* T-shirt... well, that's style!

And here's the catch, and we apologize beforehand Chi, but not *everyone* may think your T-shirt is stylish!

Hmmph!

Style is a matter of taste, and we all feel differently about things. After all, that's what makes this world an interesting place! That's why we, the authors, may love the writing of one author that you may hate. Does everyone love the Harry Potter books? We'd bet no. So, while we will teach you a bit about style and how we think you can make your writing sparkle, much of it can be a matter of opinion.

What we *can* teach you is how to get your point across. If you are doing any kind of *creative* writing, it may be okay to be subtle or to write whatever comes into your head. That would be what your teacher may call writing in a "stream of consciousness." Check this out, for example:

Leaves fall softly as the evening rain flows from the sky so blue, so cold like your eyes so hard and cruel when you left me last summer.

What the heck is this? You may like this. We'd guess a lot of you may hate it! It depends on what *style* you like. However, on no uncertain terms, whether you like this or hate this, this would *not* be acceptable writing on any essay you'd write in school. Why? Other than the fact that this is a run-on sentence, the point is not clear. You can guess that the writer is upset about some long lost love—but in academic writing, we don't leave room for guessing. In school, you not only need to write well but to write *clearly* so your ideas are understood.

Another thing we *can* teach you is how to start developing a style so that your writing has a bit more pizazz, or at the very least, emphasizes your point in a way that won't put your reader to *sleep*.

Zzzzzzzzzzzzzzzz...huh?

The point is (Thanks Chi) you need to *engage* the reader somehow. If your reader falls asleep, it doesn't matter how clear you've been. Unlike this previous passage, sentences need *direction*. The reader needs to know exactly where you are going.

Wouldn't it be simple if we could just write as we would speak? For the most part, you get through most of the day being understood, right? Unfortunately, in a conversation, sentences tend to move all over the place. And, when speaking to one another, most of us don't worry about things like Topic Sentences or Presenting Your Main Ideas! You just . . . talk, and somehow what you say is understood, at least somewhat. It's a different story when your words are put to paper.

Remember, the words and sentences are on a piece of paper all by themselves. They don't have the use of your hands or the expression in your eyes to indicate what's important or that you are being, perhaps, sarcastic. A lot is said without words, but unless you are physically there in front of your reader, a lot will be lost if you don't take care to fully express yourself. Let's take the following example:

It's eight o'clock at night. Chi's favorite show, "Buffy the Vampire Slayer," is on. She's done all her chores and finished her homework. Now she's looking forward to watching her show. Her mother asks her if she can turn off the TV and help her little brother with his math homework. She answers as follows:

"Sure, Mom. I don't have any problem with that."

Something must be wrong here. We know Chi, and there is no *way* that this could be her response! If we were there in the room, however, it might appear a little different. Maybe we can hear the irritation in her voice. Perhaps her arms are crossed and her eyes are flashing with anger and disbelief.

But, of course, we would have no way of knowing any of this. It is up to the writer to express the real meaning of Chi's words. How could we do that? Take a look at this:

> "Sure, Mom. I don't have *any* problem with that," Chi said. She looked at her brother, her eyes open and staring into him like daggers...

As you can see, although Chi's spoken words are exactly the same, the picture has changed completely. By italicizing the word *any,* the reader knows that Chi is being sarcastic. She actually has a *big* problem with helping her brother. And the next sentence makes it more than obvious that helping her brother and missing "Buffy" is not a far cry from transforming Chi into a character from *The Evil Dead*!

The point is that in order to convey your meaning in writing, you need to take control of your words and sentences. More information is needed as compared to when you speak. Let's start with the basics. There are only four types of sentences:

★ **Declarative**

★ **Imperative**

★ **Interrogative**

★ **Exclamatory**

The *declarative* sentence is the most common type you'll use (you can write entire essays with nothing but declaratives) because it simply states a fact.

Here are a few examples from Chi:

My brother is a pain in the butt. He's always
trying to tag along when I go out with my
friends. Once, he hid in the trunk of my car so he
could go to the mall with us.

The *exclamatory* sentence is just like a declarative sentence, only it's more forceful and usually ends with an exclamation point. Exclamatory sentences are more common in speeches and in creative writing.

I screamed when he popped out of the trunk!
He's lucky I didn't strangle him!

An *imperative* sentence encourages or tells the reader to do something. When you want your audience to act, as in a speech, it can be a powerful call to action:

Don't blame me for not liking my brother. You'd
hate him, too, if you ever met him.

You can also use an imperative when you want the reader to focus on a specific detail.

Consider how freaked out I was when he popped out of the trunk.

The *interrogative* sentence asks a question and always ends in a question mark. On rare occasions, you might decide to use one in your essays to introduce a new subject.

What alternatives do I have to hating my annoying little brother? Should I just ignore him? Or should I sell him to the circus and be done with it?

Just don't overuse imperatives and interrogatives in academic writing. Too many interrogatives will leave the reader wondering if you have any answers at all.

Once you figure out what you want your sentence to do (exclaim, declare, address the reader, ask a question, prance about like a pony—huh?...), you can experiment with how you build it. And that's what the rest of this chapter will explore.

Get Wise!

Decide whether each of the following sentences is declarative, imperative, interrogatory, or exclamatory.

1. My biology teacher, Ms. Weaver, has some strange eating habits. _____

2. Would you believe she likes to eat chalk? _____
_____

3. She'll be talking about something boring like DNA, when suddenly she'll pop a piece of chalk into her mouth. _____

4. The first time I saw her do it, I couldn't believe my eyes! _____

5. Once, I even saw her eat a grasshopper. _____
_____

6. It's a good thing it was already dead! _____

7. Can you imagine if it were alive? _____

8. She claims insects are a good source of protein.
_____

9. She asked the class if we wanted to share, but everyone was too grossed out! _____

10. Could you have done it? _____

11. The next time you see Ms. Weaver, ask her what she's having for lunch. _____

12. There's a good chance it'll make your stomach churn.
_____

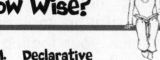
How Wise?

1. Declarative
2. Interrogative
3. Declarative
4. Exclamatory
5. Declarative
6. Exclamatory

7. Interrogative
8. Declarative
9. Exclamatory
10. Interrogative
11. Imperative
12. Declarative

SENTENCE PATTERNS

The paragraph on the next page consists primarily of humdrum sentences that repeat the same pattern:

subject – verb

(A word of warning: This paragraph is so dull, it might put you to sleep.)

Thanks for the head's up! Do you mean we may need to staple our eyelids open for this one? Ouch!

Jack was climbing the beanstalk. He didn't know what to expect since he had never done this before. His irritating mother called from below, "Watch your footing, Jackie dear!" Jack normally would have replied snottily, "Why don't you get off your butt, climb this stupid stalk, and watch my footing for me?" He kept quiet. He concentrated on his task. The stalk swayed violently beneath his weight. He tuned out his mother's voice and pulled himself up to the next branch. His only goal was to reach the top. Jack climbed the stalk carefully. He hoped it would put him out of hearing range of his nagging mother.

While this passage is clear and concise and uses vivid and concrete words, there isn't any *variety* to the sentences: *Jack was climbing. He didn't know. His irritating mother called. He kept quiet. He tuned out. Jack climbed. He hoped.* The pattern is always *subject–verb, subject–verb.* And these sentences rarely deviate from that simple structure.

We're going to show you that by simply varying your sentence structure a tiny bit, your writing will suddenly have a rhythm, and, by stressing specific information, you can cue your reader into what is most important in your sentence so that each sentence doesn't sound the same.

In other words, as the chapter title suggests, you can get your sentences to zig *and* zag, rather than just zig, zig, zig. And you can get these sentences to zig and zag where you'd like them to, rather than all over the place in no particular direction. Here are two simple tricks you can use to keep your reader from drifting off to sleep:

★ **Try combining some of the shorter sentences to form more complicated sentences.**

Instead of:

He kept quiet. He concentrated on his task. The stalk swayed violently beneath his weight.

Try:

The stalk was swaying violently beneath his weight, so he kept quiet and concentrated on his task.

★ **Change your sentence patterns around. They don't all have to start with a noun!**

Instead of:

Jack climbed the stalk carefully.

Try:

Carefully, Jack climbed the stalk.

Here's our version of the previous paragraph. Compare the two paragraphs and look at how we've changed the patterns:

Jack was climbing the beanstalk. Never having done this before, he didn't know what to expect at the top. "Watch your footing, Jackie dear!" called his irritating mother from below. Normally, Jack would have replied snottily, "Why don't you get off your butt, climb this stupid stalk, and watch my footing for me?" But the stalk was swaying violently beneath his weight, so he kept quiet and concentrated on his task. Tuning out his mother's voice, he pulled himself up to the next branch. To reach the top was his only goal. Carefully, Jack climbed the stalk. Not only did he hope it would lead him to riches and glory, he also hoped it would put him out of hearing range of his nagging mother.

Not only is it easier to read, it has something else, which makes the piece more enjoyable: style! Instead of a bunch of words and sentences thrown simply and haphazardly down on a piece of paper, the sentences work together now and have a direction or, as many writers like to call it, a "flow." The writing is smoother. And all it took was two simple tricks!

Varied Sentence Lengths

Just as you don't want to repeatedly use the same sentence patterns and structures, you don't want all of your sentences to be long or short. Short sentences call attention to themselves and quickly focus on a single point. A short sentence by itself will work to show importance. Just remember that if it is strung together with a lot of other short sentences, it loses that importance because it no longer stands out.

Long sentences, on the other hand, give you the ability to develop an idea and explore it in detail. However, long sentences also can have the annoying habit of running too long and getting out of control. So be very careful when you're using them.

Let's look at how long and short sentences can work. Read the following passages out loud. The first is a paragraph in which no sentence is longer than nine words:

Young Joe stood at the long table. Hot dogs in their buns awaited him. There were dozens of hot dogs, covered in ketchup. A paper napkin draped over his T-shirt. He looked at his competitors. They were older men, with more eating experience. They had larger stomachs and bigger appetites than Joe. Would he measure up? Could he keep pace with them? Should he even bother trying? The starting gun fired. They began eating their hot dogs, one after another. Some took large bites, while others nibbled quickly. But the boy's strategy was different. He placed one in his mouth. Then he took a sip of water. He tilted his head back. And he gulped the hot dog down whole.

Here's the same paragraph, with no sentence shorter than twenty words:

Joe's first eating competition had him lined up at a table with nine men who were much

older than he. Each man stood behind a large round platter piled high with dozens of hot dogs in soft buns and drenched with streams of juicy red ketchup that oozed over the edge. Unlike the other eaters, who didn't care if their shirts got messy with food stains, Joe wore a flimsy paper napkin over his Coney Island T-shirt. As he waited for the contest to begin, Joe sized up his opponents: they were all middle-aged men with guts grown large from many years of summer barbecues. Based on the girth of his competitors, Joe realized that the odds of his actually winning the competition were stacked up pretty high against him. Finally, the judge fired the starting pistol, and the men attacked their plates, each with a different strategy to eat more hot dogs more quickly than any other man. Some of the men crammed whole hot dogs into their mouths and chomped them down into smaller pieces before swallowing, while others took tiny but fast nibbles from their hot dogs, munching on them like bunny rabbits chewing carrots. Joe's strategy, however, was unique to the world of competitive hot dog eating in that he shoved an entire dog into his mouth, took a quick sip of water to dissolve the bun, tilted back his head until it was at a 90-degree angle to his shoulders, and, without chewing, swallowed the hot dog whole, like a pelican gulping down a fish.

Phew! Are we done yet? Guess I get your point . . . we should make our point, and fast!

The paragraphs tell the same story, but they leave the reader with two very different impressions. We had to get to the point really fast in the nine-words-or-fewer paragraph, so there wasn't much time to experiment with sentence structure—we ended up reverting to that boring old *subject-verb* pattern. Reading the paragraph out loud, you end up sounding flat and repetitive. And because all ideas are emphasized when you have nothing but short sentences, no ideas stand out from the crowd. On the other hand, the shorter sentence length allowed us to add some sentences that build suspense:

Would he measure up? Could he keep pace with them? Should he even bother trying?

It's like you are inside Joe's head, listening to him get nervous and panicked. A short sentence drives its point home.

Yeah, my mom uses those <u>short</u> sentences:
Chi, clean your room.
Chi, set the table.
Chi, do your homework.
Chi, do your homework!

In order to meet the length requirement for the second paragraph, we found ourselves combining shorter sentences and adding extra details. We mixed up the structure of our sentences, which provided variety when the paragraph was read out loud. And we were able to create drama and suspense with the longer sentences by heaping one image on top of another. But long sentences make it difficult to focus on the important information because they tend to ramble on and on, forcing the reader to dig through the words and punctuation marks to find the point.

Be careful about how you construct a long sentence. A long sentence could run on for so long that it may go right off the paper's edge and onto your desk! Okay, a bit of an exaggeration, perhaps, but the point is that a lengthy, drawn-out sentence runs the risk of losing the reader halfway through. When the reader finally reaches the period at the end, he may have no idea what you were talking about for the last forty words.

The next version of "Joe and the Hot Dog-Eating Competition" changes the rules a bit. Now, no sentence can be longer than twenty words or shorter than six, and each sentence must be at least four words longer or shorter than the sentence before it.

Joe stood at a long table, dozens of ketchup-covered hot dogs waiting on a plate in front of him. Nine men stood there with him. Each was older than Joe by at least 20 years and heavier by 40 pounds. Big Bob Williams and Harry "Hippo" Carson—these men were legendary hot dog eaters in the world of competitive eating. Joe feared that he wouldn't be able to keep up. Sweat beaded up on his forehead. The palms of his hands were wet but his mouth was dry. His stomach groaned as though it knew the gastrointestinal punishment that was about to be inflicted upon it. And then the starting gun fired. Each contestant picked up a hot dog, ketchup oozing over the bun. Some crammed a whole hot dog into their mouths at once, their cheeks puffing up like a chipmunk's. Others nibbled on hot dogs like rabbits. But Joe shoved the hot dog into his mouth, took a sip of water, and tilted his head back. Then, like a pelican, he gulped hard. The hot dog burned his throat as it slid down, slow but whole. Joe ignored the searing, hot pain. Either he would become the hot dog-eating champion of the world, or his stomach would explode in the attempt.

This version works better than the others. Changing the lengths of the sentences gave us the opportunity to experiment

with our sentence structure, which keeps the reader engaged and interested. We were able to speed things up with short, pointed sentences and slow them down with a few meandering sentences. And thanks to the word-count restrictions, we never allowed the paragraph to run out of control.

You can use these same rules for all of your writing. Here are a couple of tips for constructing sentences of different lengths:

★ **Use short sentences when you want to grab the reader's attention.**

Examples:

> Should he even bother trying?
>
> Sweat beaded up on his forehead.
>
> Then, like a pelican, he gulped hard.

★ **Don't set off unimportant ideas with short sentences because short sentences tend to stand out. And that would take away from your important idea. Combine them with other sentences.**

Examples:

Unlike the other eaters, <u>who didn't care if their shirts got messy with food stains,</u> Joe wore a flimsy paper napkin over his Coney Island T-shirt.

Each contestant picked up a hot dog, <u>ketchup oozing over the bun</u>…

★ **For long sentences, keep the subject and verb as close to the front of the sentence as possible, and then let the rest of the sentence build off of it. And don't forget to use the active voice!**

Examples:

> <u>Each man stood</u> behind a large round platter piled high with dozens of hot dogs in soft buns and drenched with streams of juicy red ketchup that oozed over the edges.

> <u>Joe's strategy, however, was unique</u> to the world of competitive hot dog eating in that he shoved an entire dog into his mouth, took a quick sip of water to dissolve the bun, tilted back his head until it was at a 90-degree angle to his shoulders, and, without chewing, swallowed the hot dog whole, like a pelican gulping down a fish.

Get Wise!

Now it's your turn to vary sentence lengths. Write several versions of a paragraph about an event in your own life. Here are some ideas:

★ Any holiday dinner with relatives (Here's a situation that guarantees an opportunity for interesting writing!)

★ School outing or event (dances, pep rallies, trip to museum)

★ Baseball game

★ Afternoon with friends at the mall

★ Baby-sitting event

★ Trip to an amusement park

Anything that involves a lot of action will work. The first time you write the paragraph, make no sentence longer than nine words. Then, rewrite it so no sentence is shorter than twenty words. Finally, write it so no sentence is shorter than six words or longer than twenty words, and each sentence is either four words longer or shorter than the one before it.

Once you've finished your three paragraphs, read them out loud. Which do you like best?

IMITATION . . .

...is the sincerest form of flattery... and it's a great way to learn how to write and develop a style! All good writers learn from other writers. Laura Ingalls Wilder may not be marking up your essays, but if you've read one of her *Little House* novels, you've learned how to string words together to paint a scene. A Stephen King horror story or a John Grisham legal thriller has taught you how to build suspense.

One of the ways aspiring writers learn to write is by imitation. So let's say you're a big fan of Ernest Hemingway's books. Hemingway's style is often described as "lean and mean." He doesn't use a lot of adjectives, and those he uses are ordinary. But somehow his sentences are vivid and to the point. They are not "fattened" up with a lot of what some consider unnecessary adjectives and description. If you enjoy direct sentences and rapid-fire dialogue, you'd like his "style." Here's an example of Hemingway's writing:

In the bed of the river there were pebbles and boulders, dry and white in the sun, and the water was clear and swiftly moving and blue in the channels.

Although his writing is simple and to the point ("In the bed of the river there were pebbles and boulders...") and his adjectives are plain ("dry and white..."), the structure of his sentence is unusual, and most striking.

Here's Chi's version, imitating Hemingway's sentence structure.

Behind the door of the closet there were clothes and shoes, heaped and wrinkled on the floor, and the laundry was dirty and rancidly stinking and fouling up the bedroom.

Do you think Chi has captured Hemingway's rhythm or style? You've got to admit that it is a pretty unusual way of describing a mess! What if you try describing that same closet with the structure of another important writer, O. Henry?

For there lay The Combs—the set of combs, side and back, that Della had worshipped for long in a Broadway window.

Here's Chi's new version.

And here sat the laundry—the pile of laundry, dirty and rancid, that David had collected for days in a bedroom closet.

Let's try one more writer you may remember from English class, good ol' Bill Shakespeare:

> But, soft! What light through yonder
>   window breaks!
> It is the east, and Juliet is the sun!

All right, let's take a deep breath and see if Chi can pull this one off.

> And, yuck! Such filth in brother's closet mounds!
> It is a sty, and David is a pig!

All right, maybe we're pushing it a little with that last one. But if you do this often enough, you'll notice three things.

1. You're going to start paying more attention to parts of speech, sentence lengths, and punctuation in your own writing.

2. You'll learn how other writers communicate their ideas through the way they craft their sentences.

3. You'll discover that your own style and voice will begin to bare a faint echo of the writers you admire most!

The more you're aware of the stylistic choices a writer makes, the more attention you'll pay to your own style. So, another good piece of advice is read, read, and read again!

Get Wise!

Try the "exercise in imitation" for yourself. Pick up books from three authors whom you admire. (We're not talking about the books that appear at the checkout line of your local Kwik-E-Mart for $4.99—pick someone who has a reputation for being a good writer and whom you've read in school, like Dickens, Steinbeck, or Twain.) Your task is to open each book to a random page and select a sentence with an unusual grammatical structure and/or sentence length. Then write a new sentence, based on the original structure and length, but with a new topic. Think of it like a complicated jigsaw puzzle: Instead of making a picture that looks like the one on the box, you will be working with pieces that have the same shapes but make a *new* picture. Following are some examples from Chi:

"Pieces of eight! Pieces of eight!"—from *Treasure Island*

"Dinner in five! Dinner in five!"

"The Rabbit started violently, dropped the white kid gloves and the fan, and skurried away into the darkness as hard as he could."—from *Alice's Adventures in Wonderland*

"Mr. Howell shouted imperially, seized the steaming blue crabs and the lobster, and settled down at the table as elegantly as he could."

"Then Rikki-tikki went out into the garden to see what was to be seen." —from *The Jungle Book*

"Then Gilligan ran over to the table to eat what was to be eaten."

Practicing the techniques in this chapter will breathe life into your writing and grab your reader's attention. It takes some practice, we'll admit, but give it a little time and perhaps a bit more practice. Also read as much as you can, and you'll find that your writing will slowly but surely start to change. Like anything else that you practice enough, there'll come a day where you don't even have to think about it and the words will start flowing naturally from your pen— in your own, unique style! But before you can build an *essay*, there's one more structural detail you need to master: the paragraph . . . or putting the sentences together!

chapter 3

Paragraphs That Work Together Stay Together

We know, you're probably wondering if we're ever going to get around to writing some real essays. We're almost there, we promise! But you can't write a masterpiece without learning some of the basics. Any great writer, or for that matter, any great artist, dancer, or composer, must start off by learning a few rules so that there is some kind of jumping-off point for being brilliant!

57

Get Wise! Mastering Writing Skills   *www.petersons.com*

Yeah, it isn't like Leonardo da Vinci just rolled out of bed one day and said, "I feel like painting the *Mona Lisa* today, even though I've never painted anything before." No, he had to practice first—with *The Last Supper.*

We're going to start this chapter with the basic . . .

You mean boring?

Ahem. . . . definition of a paragraph, which we know Chi prefers to our brilliant attempt at creating a metaphor.

Yep. You've got that right! Boring will do *juuust* fine.

A **paragraph** is a group of sentences that develops one key idea as fully as possible through supporting details. It opens with a one-sentence summary, or **topic sentence**, that explains what the topic of the paragraph will be. A good topic sentence doesn't try to do everything at once. Controlled and concise, it lays the groundwork for the discussion of a single point, preparing the reader for what is to come. The bulk of sentences in a paragraph, known as **supporting sentences**, prove the topic sentence's point—and only that point.

There is no hard and fast rule to how long your paragraphs should be, but there are a couple of general guidelines to keep in mind:

* ★ Always start a new paragraph when it's time to discuss a new idea.

* ★ Break up a long paragraph into two or more smaller paragraphs.

* ★ Combine paragraphs of closely related ideas when they are too short to stand on their own.

* ★ Keep all paragraphs about the same length. Otherwise, your reader might subconsciously believe a longer paragraph is more important simply because of its length.

THE TOPIC SENTENCE

A topic sentence needs to do one important thing: Catch the reader's attention. If it's dull and vague, the reader won't bother to continue reading. What's the difference between a good topic sentence and a bad one? Well, here's a bad one (from our trusted sidekick, you know who!):

This paragraph examines a vegetable.

This poor excuse for a topic sentence certainly explains that a vegetable will be discussed, but it leaves the reader with too many questions. What kind of vegetable? A carrot? A pea? And what about this vegetable will be examined? And why would one want to read about this anyway? How can a paragraph about a vegetable be of interest to anyone? The more concrete and specific you make your topic sentence, the better its chances of being a good topic sentence *and* intriguing your reader.

Topic sentences fall into three categories: direct, indirect, and rhetorical. Let's look at Chi's **direct** sentence, which states exactly what will happen in the paragraph:

The most intense vegetable I've ever eaten is a jalapeño pepper.

Not only does the reader now know what to expect from the rest of the paragraph—an examination of a specific vegetable—he is fed just enough detail in the topic sentence to be hooked. How can a vegetable be intense? If he's eaten the vegetable in question, he's already thinking about his own experiences, which most likely are equally intense. (Jalapeños do tend to create intense eating experiences!) He is likely to continue reading to see why *you* feel it is the most intense. Even if the reader has never eaten a jalapeño, he's going to be intrigued by your topic sentence ("A whole sketch about an intense vegetable? I've got to read more!").

The **indirect** topic sentence, on the other hand, is, well, indirect. It doesn't flat-out say what the topic is:

The other day, I ate an intense vegetable.

The sentence hints at what the paragraph will be about— an intense vegetable—but rather than provide details about what was so intense, it acts as a hook, leaving the reader wanting to know what made the vegetable so intense. The paragraph's supporting sentences will fill in the details.

Finally, there is the **rhetorical** topic sentence, which poses a question to the reader:

How intense is a jalapeño pepper?

Like the direct and indirect sentences, the rhetorical topic sentence sets up the paragraph's topic, and the remaining sentences of the paragraph will, hopefully, answer the question of just how intense the vegetable is.

There are no strict rules to deciding which kind of topic sentence to use in a paragraph. Here, however, are a few general guidelines:

★ Stick with the direct topic sentence when you haven't got a lot of time to write your essay, like when you're taking a timed essay test. The direct sentence will let you get to your main ideas quickly.

★ Indirect topic sentences are great for personal essays when your writing can be more informal and you have more time.

★ Rhetorical topic sentences work best when you're writing an essay that actually addresses the reader, like in a personal essay or an argumentative essay. (Argumentative essays are the type you write when you want to convince your reader that you're right and everyone else is wrong about a topic of debate.)

Spend a little extra time crafting your topic sentences because they're the best tool you've got for drawing your reader into a paragraph. If you lose your reader here, you might as well call it a day and stick your paper in the shredder! Use vivid and concrete language (don't forget everything we talked about in Chapter 1) so the reader knows exactly what you're going to discuss in your paragraph. And make sure that your topic sentence contains a solid idea that is worth exploring further in your paragraph.

SUPPORTING SENTENCES

Once you've created your topic sentence, you're ready to create the **supporting sentences**, which will build upon the topic. Each of these sentences must connect back to the point of your topic sentence, as well as enhance it. Don't let your supporting sentences veer off into new directions. As you write, keep your topic sentence in mind, and ask yourself if each sentence either explains or supports the topic. In other words, if your paragraph is about the first time you saw your grandmother's dentures, don't swerve off course and talk about the most popular denture adhesives on the market. The following paragraph supports our topic sentence, but we inserted a few sentences that went off in another direction and ruined the "flow." In other words, despite the fact that they still talk about the subject at hand, these sentences take the reader away from the main point.

Get Wise!

Underline the irrelevant supporting sentences in the following paragraph:

The first time I ate a jalapeño pepper, I thought my mouth would explode. Jalapeños are often used in Mexican cuisine. I knew the pepper would be hot, but I didn't expect the heat to linger for so long. Beads of perspiration formed on my forehead, trickled down my temples, and soaked the collar of my shirt. Even though I drank three glasses of water, it took a good five minutes before I was able to cool down. Removing the seeds lessens the effects of the heat. Despite the discomfort I experienced from that first pepper, I couldn't help but eat a second. The peppers are especially good when you stuff them with melted cheddar cheese.

How Wise?

Jalapeños are often used in Mexican cuisine.

Removing the seeds lessens the effects.

The peppers are especially good when you stuff them with melted cheddar cheese.

Let's see how it reads now when we stick to our point.

The first time I ate a jalapeño pepper, I thought my mouth would explode. I knew the pepper would be hot, but I didn't expect the heat to linger for so long. Beads of perspiration formed on my forehead, trickled down my temples, and soaked the collar of my shirt. Even though I drank three glasses of water, it took a good five minutes before I was able to cool down. Despite the discomfort I experienced from that first pepper, I couldn't help but eat a second.

TRANSITIONAL PHRASES: THE ART OF CONNECTING SENTENCES

Transitional words and phrases join ideas. Without them, your essay will be a mishmash of sentences, which makes it hard for the reader to follow the progression of thoughts or events in your paragraph. Sentences that are carefully connected by transitions, however, lead the reader naturally along the way through the paragraph. We're sure you already know what transitions look like, but just to refresh your memory, here are a few examples:

> **to show addition:** and, next, too, also
>
> **to show physical movement:** above, below, around the corner
>
> **give examples:** for example, specifically
>
> **to compare:** also, likewise
>
> **to contrast:** but, however, on the other hand, even though
>
> **to conclude:** in summary, therefore
>
> **to show time:** finally, first, meanwhile
>
> **to show cause or effect:** for this reason, as a result, therefore

Take a look at the transitions in the following paragraph:

> It wouldn't feel like an American summer without the adrenaline rush of a death-defying ride on a turning, plummeting, loop-de-looping roller coaster. **However,** the great American scream machine isn't an American innovation. **In fact,** it origi-

nated in Russia more than 600 years ago. **Early in the fifteenth century,** Russians dove down ice-covered hills on simple wooden sleds, enjoying the rush of speed in the midst of the slow, long-lasting winter. **By the 1600s,** nobles in St. Petersburg (including Catherine the Great) were building hills—steep and rickety wooden structures coated with thick layers of ice—for their personal use. **In order to provide the most speed,** ramps were shaped like skateboarding ramps, stood between 70 and 80 feet in height, and stretched for hundreds of feet in length.

Each transition moves the reader along the structure of the paragraph, as well as helps keep track of the events that the paragraph speaks about.

Get Wise!

Write a paragraph in which you describe the last vacation you took with your family. Use transitional words and phrases to show the progression of thoughts and events. Chi's paragraph is on the following page:

Last summer, my parents took my brother, sister, and me to the beach for a weeklong vacation. **Normally**, our vacations are disasters. **Of course**, this trip was no exception. **On the first day**, my sister caught sun poisoning. **So** she spent the rest of the week indoors. **Then**, I was stung by a jellyfish. **For two days**, I had to keep a raw steak pressed against my ankle. **Finally**, my brother went water skiing. **But** he's a klutz and ended up breaking his leg. **As a result of these catastrophes**, the three of us have refused to ever go away on a family vacation again.

PARAGRAPH STRUCTURE

There's one other thing you need to think about when you're writing a paragraph: How are you going to arrange your sentences? You can't just slap down a bunch of supporting sentences and expect them to prove the point of your topic sentence. They need to be placed in a logical manner that develops the idea you're trying to prove. Here are five of the most popular methods of organization.

Example

Pick the examples that best prove your topic sentence. Start with your least important example and build up to your most important example. This gives you more bang for your buck—the reader comes away from the paragraph with the strongest piece of evidence freshest in his or her mind. Don't use just one example because the reader won't be convinced that you've proven your point. Also don't use too many examples, or else the reader will be overwhelmed by the information overload and may forget what your point was in the first place! Anywhere from two to four examples in a paragraph should be good enough. Take a look at Chi's example:

The worst summer job I ever had was when I was a camp counselor. [TOPIC SENTENCE] We were supposed to spend most of our time outside, hiking, horseback riding, and swimming. But it rained all July and August, which made it impossible to do any of that. The kids were pretty well-behaved, but I had one kid who was so homesick that he screamed and cried all day long, giving me a three-week headache! The worst part of the job, however, occurred three days before we all went home. I fell into a patch of poison ivy and ended up with a nasty rash all over my face, legs, and hands. It didn't clear up until late September. I'll never work at that camp again!

This paragraph presents three examples of what made this the worst summer job:

1. It rained.

2. One kid cried the whole time.

3. The poison ivy.

Of the three examples, the third will probably make the strongest impact on the reader, so it's been placed at the end of the paragraph.

Narration

In a narrative paragraph, your supporting sentences will tell a story in chronological order. Here's Chi's example:

I was late for school this morning. [TOPIC SENTENCE] First, my brother thought it would be funny to turn off my alarm clock while I was sleeping, so I didn't wake up on time. Then, my mother decided to run the washing machine, so I had to wait half an hour before there was enough water for me to take a shower. As if that weren't bad enough, I couldn't find my history homework. It turns out, my sister had packed it in her backpack by accident. And then I spent another ten minutes chasing the dog all over the neighborhood because my dad forgot to close the gate to our backyard. If it hadn't been for my family, I never would have missed the school bus this morning.

Compare/Contrast

Comparing draws attention to similarities between two items. *Contrasting* draws attention to differences between two items. This is a great method to use when you're writing about the pros and cons of an issue or two literary characters. Make sure your topic sentence clearly states at the beginning of your paragraph which two items you're going to be comparing or contrasting, though. Otherwise, the reader will think she's reading about one thing and become confused when you suddenly jump into a discussion of something else. Also, make sure you compare or contrast *similar* points. This is our favorite example from Chi, of course!

Broccoli provides a more enjoyable dining experience than peas. **[TOPIC SENTENCE]** You can quickly spear a piece of broccoli with your fork or pick it up with your fingers. Peas, however, frustrate the diner by rolling all over the plate. Also, broccoli looks like a tree, with a trunk and leaves, and can be arranged in different ways on the plate. Peas, on the other hand, are visually unappealing wrinkled balls. Finally, broccoli offers the diner two distinct tastes: the sweetness of the stalk and the bitterness of the crunchy, leafy top. No matter what part of the pea you bite into, the taste is always the same—bland and uninteresting.

Cause and Effect

A cause-and-effect structure is similar to an example paragraph. The only difference is that the topic sentence is your cause, and the examples are the effects of the cause.

My little sister Ellen wanted a clown at her birthday party, but Mom hired a magician instead. [TOPIC SENTENCE—THE CAUSE] When the magician arrived, Ellen threw a temper tantrum and ran up to her bedroom. Mom spent most of the afternoon pounding on Ellen's locked bedroom door, screaming at her to come out. Dad stayed in the kitchen, wondering if anyone would notice if he cut a piece of the cake for himself. My brother, of course, was no help at all. He retreated to his best friend's house. This left me alone with a bunch of six-year-olds and an unwanted magician. It turns out that this was supposed to be the magician's first public performance ever. But he was so upset by my sister's reaction that he hung up his wand and top hat, sat down at our kitchen table, and cried.

Definition

A definition paragraph lets you clarify or explain the meaning of a term, phrase, or concept. Don't use it to define something that can be found easily in the dictionary, like *Siamese cat*. Instead, use it for abstract or more complicated terms that can't be explained in just a sentence or two, such as *love* or *quantum physics*. Your topic sentence should state what you're going to define, and the supporting sentences can follow the organization of any of the previous types of paragraphs. You can list **examples** or **narrate** a story to illustrate what you're defining. Or you can **compare** it to or **contrast** it against something that the reader might already be familiar with. Let's look at Chi's example as she defines mud-sledding:

To alleviate stress while studying for final exams, many college students take to the hills for a few rounds of "mud-sledding." [TOPIC SENTENCE] First, the students must "borrow" a tray from the school cafeteria, either hiding it in their backpacks or creating a diversion so the staff doesn't catch them. Then, they must change into T-shirts and shorts that they don't mind getting a little dirty and climb to the top of the tallest hill on campus. If the students are lucky, a steady and hard rain will be falling. Otherwise, they must hook up a hose and drench the hill themselves. Once the hillside is covered in a thick layer of muddy ooze, the students slide down on their cafeteria trays. The wetter the ground, the faster the slide.

Get Wise!

Try your hand at writing paragraphs that follow each organizational structure we've shown you. Here are a few topics you might want to consider:

1. **Example:** What is your favorite holiday, and why?

2. **Narration:** Describe what happens in the last ten minutes of your favorite movie.

3. **Compare/Contrast:** Compare or contrast the personalities of two of your friends.

4. **Cause and Effect:** What are the side effects of keeping a messy bedroom?

5. **Definition:** Explain to a person from another culture a sport you enjoy participating in or watching.

chapter 4

Methods of Madness
(or How to Brainstorm)

I bet you thought we were ready to start writing some essays. Well, we still have one more very important topic to cover before we move on to crafting the essay. We think you'll be glad we took you through this. How often have you sat in front of a piece of paper with absolutely no idea of what to write? It's like your brain went into freeze mode. Ideas rarely, if ever, magically appear like a light bulb over your head. Even if something pops into your head as soon as you sit down to write your essay, it's unlikely you'll get far without thinking about if for a little while. The prompt may be simple, but the thoughts are just not coming! This is when the Dreaded Writer's Block sets in.

You know what that means. Nausea, panic attacks, sweaty palms, and an overwhelming fear that you'll never finish your essay. And adults wonder why teens are so moody and miserable!

There's no reason to ever feel that way. We've got a couple of surefire ways to ensure you'll never experience brain freeze again!

FIND YOUR THESIS STATEMENT

If you're lucky, a few electrical charges will go off in your brain, and you'll have a faint idea of what you want to write about. If, however, nothing comes to you, at least one of the following methods are guaranteed to start the sparks flying! So, now you can relax and try some of these with us:

Listing

Look at your prompt, and WITHOUT THINKING, yes, you heard us right, without thinking, make a list of everything that pops into your head that has to do with your subject. Don't worry about putting the items in order, making them grammatically correct, or focusing on which ideas are strong or weak, smart or stupid. Just write down *whatever* comes to mind. Once you've got a decent-size list, go back and see if any of the ideas stand out as potential thesis statements for your essay. Here's a sample prompt for this listing method:

PROMPT—If your best friend were asked what your three worst qualities are, what would she say?

★ Ears too big
★ Too bossy
★ Talk too much
★ Bite fingernails
★ Dance like Elaine on *Seinfeld*

Now, look back at the prompt, and this time you have to think a little (sorry!) and then back at your list. Do any of the items have any potential to work as a thesis statement? That would be one great big sentence that tells you what your entire essay is about. We'll explain it in more detail in Chapter 5. Chances are there's a germ of an idea in one or two of the items you listed. We elect "Too bossy" from Chi's list. While that in itself is too simple to work as a thesis statement, it can be expanded. "Too bossy" can eventually be worked into a discussion on, say, how you may not be sensitive to other's feelings— or something similar to that. The point is the exercise got your brain to unfreeze and start thinking about your qualities. Note: We'd probably delete the first and last bullet as *we* don't think these are important qualities that a good friend should consider.

Freewriting

This is similar to listing, but here you are not even trying to be logical. This is for ultra-brain-freeze! Set aside ten minutes to write down *whatever is in your head* about the subject. It may not make sense when you read it later, but don't worry—no one will read it except you. Once time is up, you'll probably have a good sense of where you stand on the subject, and you might even be able to pull out a few gems and use them in your essay. Here's the prompt:

PROMPT—Should school start later in the day?

And here's Chi's freewrite:

Duh! I hate waking up before dawn to catch the bus. Unnatural to expect a person to roll outta bed before the sun rises. Always cold. Never enough time to eat breakfast. Takes so long to do homework at night that I'm always yawning in my first two or three classes the next day. Last week, Brian fell asleep in second period history class. Kendall's always so grumpy early in the morning. Michelle's always late for school because she sleeps through her alarm clock. Parents don't start work until 9. Why should I have to be at school by 7:30 when I'm not even getting paid to go there? ...

Is there anything here that Chi could use and expand on? If you look back at the freewrite, what comes to light is the fact that there is not a lot of time to get enough sleep. Chi can now focus on the time factor and that kids need more sleep to have a more productive day at school. The point is if you relax and start writing, the ideas will start to come.

Asking Questions: Who, What, Where, When, Why, and How?

This is an excellent and easy method for getting the ball rolling. Always resort to this one when nothing else works. A newspaper article always answers six questions: Who? What? Where? When? Why? and How? Try it yourself and see if any of your answers lead you to a thesis. Here's your prompt:

PROMPT—It's pretty likely these days that either you or someone you know is a vegetarian. Write an essay about why someone decided to become a vegetarian.

When did they become a vegetarian?

Why did they decide to do so?

Where were they when they made this decision?

Who are the vegetarians of this world?

How do vegetarians eat?

What do vegetarians say are their reasons for not eating meat?

Almost any of these would work as a thesis statement once they were expanded on. Let's look at *Where*, for example. Perhaps you or someone you know was reading an article about how they slaughter cows when the decision was made. It would then be easy to lead into a thesis statement such as:

In 1999, I read an article in *Newsweek* about the slaughtering of cows. It filled me with such disgust that right then and there, I knew I could never eat meat again.

Not bad. Asking questions almost always works like a charm.

Get Wise!

Use one of the above methods to come up with a thesis statement based on the following question:

PROMPT—Are rock stars born or made?

Chi's freewrite:

I suppose rock stars are a result of the media, groomed by handlers and PR reps to fit the teen market. Grow their hair long. Cut their hair short. Go on a diet. Get plastic surgery. Become camera-friendly. What would they have done to Janis Joplin to make her camera-friendly? Would she have even been given a recording contract since she wasn't a size 6 blond with perfect skin? All about videos and promotion now. Learn to dance for big televised concerts. Take acting lessons so they can make videos. Trained like dolphins to behave in specific way for the press. Not like the early days of rock, when rock stars didn't care about making the media happy. Remember that scene in The Doors movie when they were on the Ed Sullivan show, and the exec told them to change the lyrics? Jim Morrison said ok, but then when they performed live, he still said "Girl we couldn't get much higher." What's the likelihood of an emerging rock star doing the same thing today? Well, maybe Marilyn Manson, but even his shocking behavior is planned, appealing to a specific market...

Guess I know where I stand on this one! Rock stars are made, not born.

PROVING YOUR THESIS STATEMENT

Once you know what you want to prove, you have to figure out how you're going to prove it. Your brainstorming will be more focused now, and the method you use will depend a lot on how much time you've got to write your essay and what kind of essay you need to write.

Bubbles

The bubble method works best for timed essays. The following pages will take you through it, step by step. Say you're given the following prompt:

Should students be required to attend gym class during the school day?

Using one of the previous brainstorming methods, you come up with the thesis statement,

"Students should not be required to attend gym class during the school day."

Now write that sentence it in the center of your paper and draw a circle around it. Then write down and circle every word and idea that comes to mind about your thesis in the space around it, as well as words that you associate with each of your bubbles. Depending on how much time you've got to write your essay, you might want to limit the bubbling to a few minutes. If time isn't a factor (say, you've got a couple of days to write your essay), keep bubbling until you can't think of another word. Here's what we came up with (see next page):

Chart 1

Your books smell like your gym locker

Lifting weights

Gym is boring

Gym class involves dangerous activities

Rough games like dodge ball

Gross-smelling mats and gym equipment

Students should not gym class during the sc

Get an "F" if you can't do a chin-up or run the mile in less than 9 minutes

P.E. teachers usually favor the school's varsity athletes to pick teams

Non-jocks sit around and do nothing when teacher isn't watching

Gym clothes smell really gross by end of semester

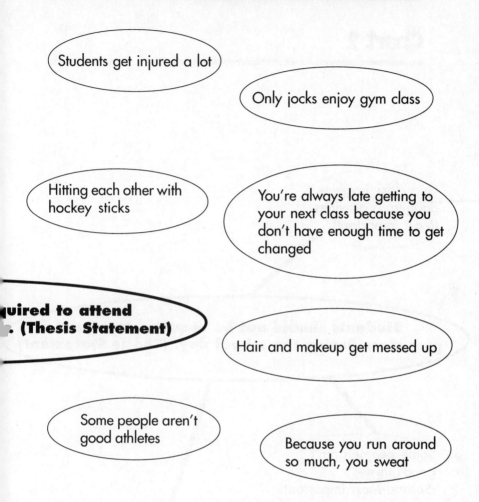

Students get injured a lot

Only jocks enjoy gym class

Hitting each other with hockey sticks

You're always late getting to your next class because you don't have enough time to get changed

quired to attend . (Thesis Statement)

Hair and makeup get messed up

Some people aren't good athletes

Because you run around so much, you sweat

Whether time's up or you're out of ideas, take a look at your bubbles and choose at least three of the bubbles that stand out from the rest, as though they might be the main ideas of individual paragraphs. Underline those bubbles and decide which are the most important, the second-most important, and the least important (we'll call these "main bubbles"). The main bubbles will form the topic sentences of your supporting paragraphs. Draw branches between the main bubbles and the thesis bubble.

Chart 2

Gym class involves
dangerous activities
(Most Important)

Students should not be required to attend
gym class during the school day. (Thesis Statement)

Some people aren't
good athletes
(Second-Most Important)

Because you run around
so much, you sweat
(Third-Most Important)

Next, decide which of the remaining bubbles support each of your main ideas (we'll call them "support bubbles"). For each support bubble, draw a branch that connects it to its main bubble. These bubbles will become the details that prove your topic sentences. Any bubbles that you can't branch to your thesis or topic bubbles are probably going to be irrelevant to your thesis. Delete them out and forget about them. Then number the supporting detail bubbles in the order they'll appear in each paragraph. With the bubble and branch method, there's no need to write a formal outline. Your chart will do the trick:

Chart 3

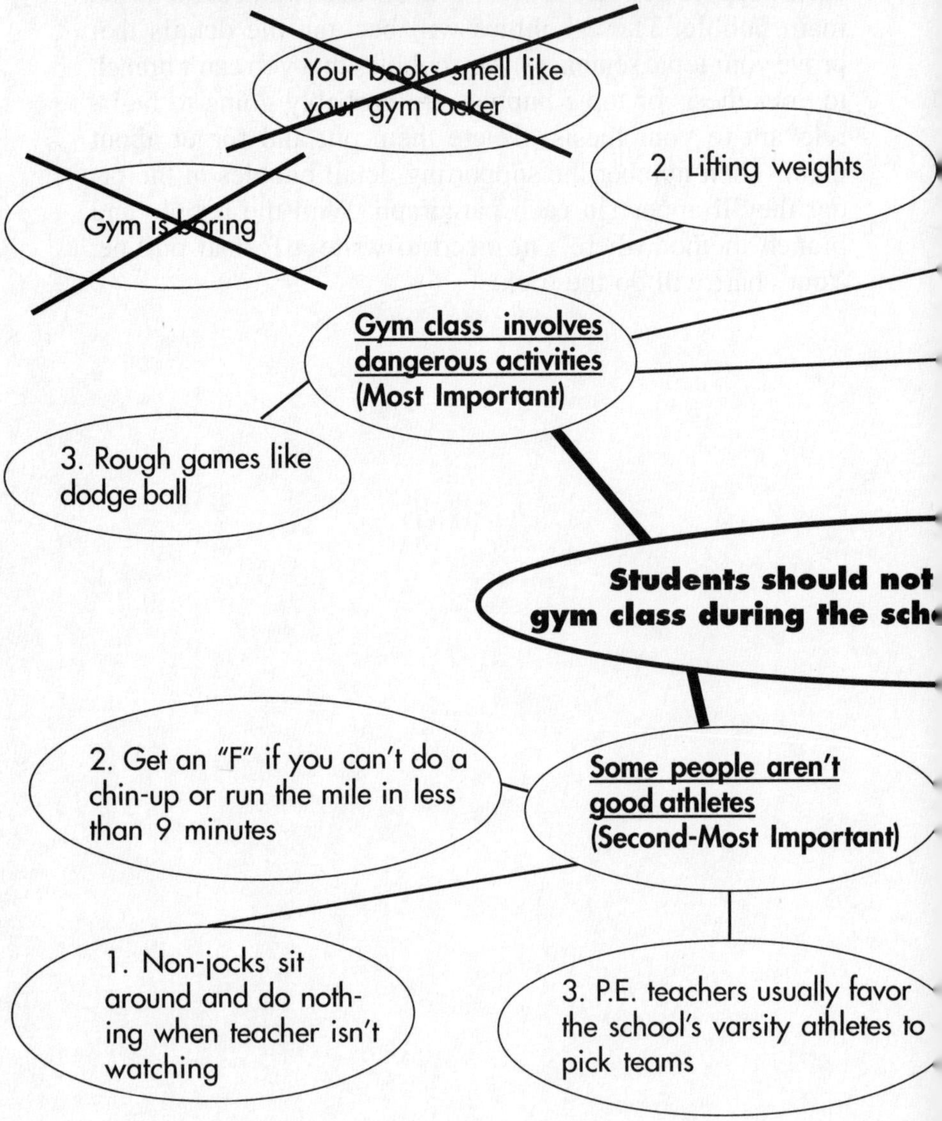

Your books smell like your gym locker

2. Lifting weights

Gym is boring

Gym class involves dangerous activities (Most Important)

3. Rough games like dodge ball

Students should not gym class during the sch

2. Get an "F" if you can't do a chin-up or run the mile in less than 9 minutes

Some people aren't good athletes (Second-Most Important)

1. Non-jocks sit around and do nothing when teacher isn't watching

3. P.E. teachers usually favor the school's varsity athletes to pick teams

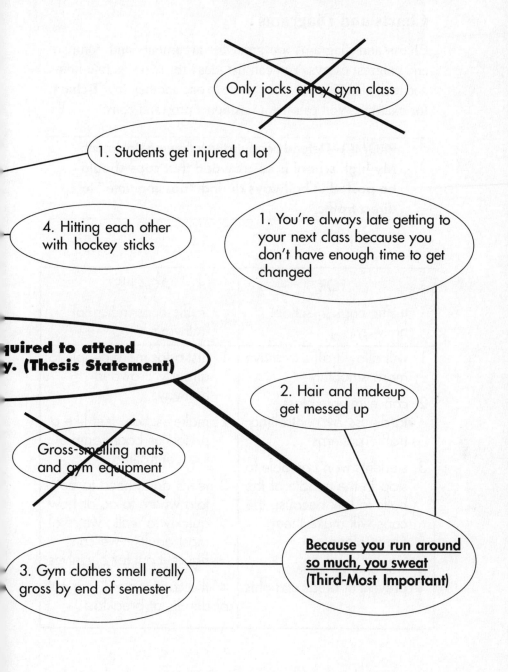

Only jocks enjoy gym class

1. Students get injured a lot

4. Hitting each other with hockey sticks

1. You're always late getting to your next class because you don't have enough time to get changed

...quired to attend ...y. (Thesis Statement)

Gross-smelling mats and gym equipment

2. Hair and makeup get messed up

3. Gym clothes smell really gross by end of semester

Because you run around so much, you sweat (Third-Most Important)

Charts and Diagrams

Charts and diagrams are great for arguments and compare and contrast essays. You can list ideas for two separate items and then visualize how they relate to one another. In a **T chart**, for example, you can list a position's pros and cons:

PROMPT—Defend or refute the following statement: My high school is so crowded that cops should be posted in hallways during "passing time" to direct traffic.

FOR traffic cops in school hallways	AGAINST traffic cops in school hallways
1. will allow traffic to move more smoothly 2. can eliminate class tardiness by controlling traffic patterns 3. students won't be able to stop in the middle of the halls to talk because the cops will make them move along 4. will also be able to prevent or break up fights	1. just adds more people to already crowded hallways 2. makes school feel like a prison or boot camp—too controlling 3. teens don't need to be told where to go or how quickly to walk; we're al most adults—we can figure it out for ourselves 4. the cafeteria will run out of donuts at breakfast

Venn diagrams allow you to compare and contrast two or more subjects. If you're lucky, you'll find similarities (list them where the circles overlap) and differences:

PROMPT—Students often complain that the food served in the high school cafeteria is worse than dog food. Do you agree or disagree?

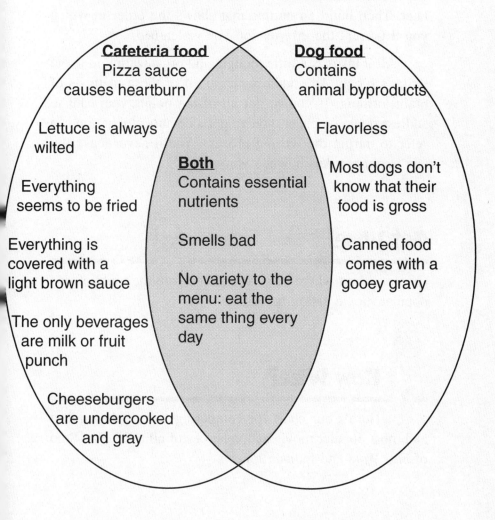

<u>**Cafeteria food**</u>
Pizza sauce causes heartburn

Lettuce is always wilted

Everything seems to be fried

Everything is covered with a light brown sauce

The only beverages are milk or fruit punch

Cheeseburgers are undercooked and gray

<u>**Both**</u>
Contains essential nutrients

Smells bad

No variety to the menu: eat the same thing every day

<u>**Dog food**</u>
Contains animal byproducts

Flavorless

Most dogs don't know that their food is gross

Canned food comes with a gooey gravy

Research

If you don't know much (if anything) about your subject, crack open a couple of books, connect to the Web, look through back issues of magazines, or watch a couple of movies—learn whatever you can about your subject. You should be able to find all of these resources at your local library. Take notes and pull out pieces of support for your thesis later. Then build an outline that shows the order in which you'll present the information you've learned.

All it takes is a little thought and organization to avoid writer's block. An added bonus to all of these methods of brainstorming: If you've got all of the points you want to address down on paper, you've got a document that you can refer to during the writing process. You'll never leave out any important details when you write!

Get Wise!

Create a chart where you list and compare the traits of two popular movie action heroes.

How Wise?

Here's our chart for comparing two of the coolest and most popular movie action heroes of all time, Han Solo of *Star Wars* and Indiana Jones:

Traits in common	Han Solo	Indiana Jones
Ingenuity	• "It's all a lot of simple tricks and nonsense." • Attaches Falcon to side of Imperial cruiser • Pretends to be Imperial soldier to get in shield generator	• Uses raft to escape airplane • Pretends he's Scottish art expert to get in castle
Fearless	• Chases squad of storm troopers even though he's outnumbered • Enters asteroid field • Leads team to infiltrate shield generator	• Chases truck on horseback • Cuts rope bridge • Flies airplane even though he doesn't know how to land
Risks life to save others	• Returns to help Luke blow up Death Star • Searches for Luke despite dropping temperatures	• Swims after Marion, who is prisoner on a submarine • Frees the children from the Temple of Doom • Faces final challenge of the Grail to save his father

If you would like to see the essay we prepared based on this brainstorm, go to page 201 in the Appendix of this book.

chapter 5

Chi and The Fab 5 (or How to Create an Essay in 5 Easy Pieces)

The Fab 5? Sound like a rock group? Well, okay, maybe from your parents' era... In any case, if you look at our 5 Easy Pieces (or 5-paragraph plan) for creating a basic essay, you'll see how the rock band analogy plays out. In the same way that the guitar player, bass player, keyboarder, drummer, and lead singer each play a separate instrument and contribute a certain sound to the overall harmony of the group, each of the 5 paragraphs "plays" a certain role and contributes to the overall idea of the writing piece. In the

95

Get Wise! Mastering Writing Skills　　　　www.petersons.com

rock band, it is the singer who leads the group, and she is the one who everyone has their eyes (and ears) on during a performance. In the essay, it is YOUR VOICE that leads the writing piece, and that is what your teachers will have their eye (and ear) on as they grade your performance!

Chi and The Fab 5? Are you talkin' to *me*? Give me a break! Uh…yeah, sure, brilliant … I think we're getting a little desperate here—using lame rock band analogies to get us to pay attention! Whatever…

Sorry Chi. We will try anything. But whether you like our analogy or not, our 5-paragraph plan really works! And we did promise we'd give you a foolproof plan that you can use for any prompt that could come up in school. Let's check it out:

Chi and The Fab 5

Easy Piece 1: The Intro

Easy Piece 2: First Support Paragraph

Easy Piece 3: Second Support Paragraph

Easy Piece 4: Third Support Paragraph

Easy Piece 5: Conclusion

As you can see, there really isn't much to it! It's just an introduction, three paragraphs of support, and a conclusion. You already know how to pull a few tricks with words, sentences, and paragraphs to impress your teachers. The tough part's over. Now it's just a matter of putting it all together and into the outline you see on page 96. And once you've got this format firmly planted in your head, anything you'll ever have to write will be a piece of cake! You'll wonder what all the fuss was about! So, let's start with the intro.

EASY PIECE 1: THE INTRO

The introduction (better known as "the intro") will be your teacher's first impression so it's important to get this right. First, it has to… **"State Your Position."** Now that may sound difficult, but it's really only about picking a side: Are you pro or con? You don't have to worry about insulting your reader. Take only one position and stay with it. If your prompt is not about agreeing or disagreeing with a statement, then it will simply tell the reader what the essay is about. Second, and more important, it has to capture the reader's attention so that he or she actually wants to read the thing! Finally, a good intro should pave the way for the rest of your thoughts, letting them flow smoothly all the way through to the conclusion.

Huh? Yeah, sure. Simply this and simply that… Sounds like *a lot* to accomplish in a single paragraph! Actually, it sounds more like a recurring nightmare! Blank sheets of paper chase me down the halls of my school, screaming at me to fill them with words!

OK, Chi, take a chill pill! We did promise we would make this easy for you, and we shall. We *can* accomplish all of the above in one simple step. How do we do that? We do that by creating . . . **The Thesis Statement** (remember that?), which will do all of the above and more!

A quick reminder: Back when we looked at building paragraphs, we saw how a strong **topic sentence** sets the foundation for the rest of its **paragraph**. It keeps the writer focused on a single topic and clearly defines what the paragraph is going to be about. The **thesis statement** works in the same way, but on a much larger scale. Instead of keeping a single paragraph in focus, it works for the **entire essay** and explains how you'll prove your position. That is the true purpose of our intro—<u>to house the thesis statement</u>.

If you still don't have a good hold on how to create a thesis statement, or if we have not held you completely spellbound, and you've been skipping pages, go back now and review Chapter 4. It is important to know how to brainstorm and create your thesis statement and topic sentences beforehand.

So, let's say Chi has been given the following prompt for a writing assignment:.

PROMPT—Defend or refute the following: School should start later in the day.

As you learned in the previous chapter, the first step is brainstorming. Whether Chi has decided to use the list method, freewriting, bubbling, or diagramming, she now has a main point she will pull from her notes. She's not going to worry if it is grammatically correct or perfectly structured. For now, we are just setting up the *first draft*. The fine-

tuning or *editing* comes later, and we'll go over that in another chapter . . . you can even watch TV in between!

Here's Chi's thesis statement:

School starts much too early
in the morning. Kids keep
falling asleep in class. The
fact is their days and nights
are so jam-packed with
activities that they can't get
to sleep at a decent hour.
It's totally abnormal, and it's
turning them into zombies!

Has Chi done what needs to be done? Well, we certainly know her position on the matter of when school should
start. Chi believes on no uncertain terms that school starts
way too early, and she feels pretty strongly that this is a
major problem!

As you can see, the thesis statement doesn't have to be
limited to a single sentence. Although Chi's done it in four,
she is concise and to the point. She says nothing more and
nothing less than what she means. Remember, this is not
creative writing. All your teacher will care about is if you
can put your thoughts together in a logical and coherent
way.

Chi's thesis statement begins by . . . that's right, stating her position. That's it. Simple! However, instead of simply repeating words from the prompt ("School should start
later in the day"), she states her position by turning the words

around: "School starts much too early in the morning." You should know, however, that even if Chi *had* repeated the prompt word-for-word exactly like a parrot, that would be OK, too—as long as you are clear about where you stand on your position. That is all that counts.

Additionally, and this is important, we are not so worried about your style or choice of words just yet. The purpose of this chapter and the 5-paragraph plan is to get your thoughts organized into a proper structure. We'll worry about grammar, spelling, word choice, and all that stuff when we get to editing in Chapter 6. So, sit back, relax, and . . . well, maybe sit up a bit! The point is to take this one step at a time, and right now we're not going to worry about that.

So back to our first paragraph. The rest of Chi's thesis statement simply adds some facts (*kids keep falling asleep . . . days and nights are jam-packed with activities . . . can't get to sleep at a decent hour*), which she should have been able to pull from whatever brainstorming method she decided to use. The last part of her thesis statement makes a strong comment about the situation ("It is totally abnormal . . .") *and* it makes a prediction ("It's turning them into a zombies.").*

So far nothing's too complicated here, right? Choose a position, state it clearly, then throw in some details so you can use each one (three in this case) as a Topic Sentence for your next three supporting paragraphs. Remember, the three supporting paragraphs need to do just that—support the main thesis statement. Don't worry, we'll show you how that works later. Thanks to the thesis statement, the reader now knows what to expect, and Chi has a plan to follow when she constructs the rest of the essay.

---

* *Making a prediction is a catchy intro tip, which we will get into later.*

A Catchy Intro

Before we go on to the supporting paragraphs, we're going to take a break and focus on how to create a catchy intro and grab your reader's attention. Chi used one of them in the last part of her thesis statement. She made a *prediction*. Let's look at that:

Make a Prediction

Chi said:

">. . . It's turning them into zombies."

When you make a prediction, you are presenting the reader with an ending, sort of like when you watch a movie and it's told in flashback. You watch the movie to find out how they arrived at that final scene. In the same way, the reader will read on and figure out how you got to your prediction. In this case, the reader might think it's one thing to want to go to school later, but why would students turn into zombies? They would have to read the essay to find out.

Chi's first detail statement, "Kids keep falling asleep in class," was simple but clear. What if we turned that into a question?

Ask a Question

What if Chi asked:

"Is it any wonder kids keep falling asleep in class?"

Asking a question creates suspense on the part of the reader. Again, the reader is lured into reading on. But can this work for any prompt? Let's try a more serious prompt, more like you would get in class. Respond to the following:

PROMPT—Are Americans doing all they can do to protect the environment?

Yawn! You're right about that . . . sure does sound like something I would get in class . . .

Sorry, but we need to show how this works with a prompt you may actually get from your teacher. Let's try creating a thesis statement where we ask a question:

Isn't our environment becoming uninhabitable?

It sounds scary, doesn't it? What kind of environment would be uninhabitable? The reader, again, has to read on to find out! We think you probably get the picture by now, and we will give you some more practice later on. Let's move on to . . .

Challenge an Established Idea

This one's easy, but it works because you will most likely be saying the opposite of what the reader expects. Therefore, you arouse the reader's curiosity. Let's see how this works with our original prompt: **School Should Start Later in the Day**. Chi will help us out here:

Kids have been dragging their @##%# out of bed for decades in order to get to school by 7:30 A.M. We would all be A+ students if we could start school at noon.

Note from the authors: Under no circumstances should you use curse words or symbols that stand for curse words for any writing you do in school! Nor should you use offensive words as we *might have* done here. We're just trying to have some fun with you, but remember, this will not score points with your teachers nor anyone else for that matter.

Okay, back to challenging an established idea. When was the last time you heard that it would be good for a student to start school at noon? And that students would *excel* by doing so? You kind of want to hear what Chi has to say. How is she going to prove that going to school at noon will produce A+ students? You'd have to read on. So, the idea is to make your intro and your thesis statement *compelling*, to lure the reader into your thoughts.

A note about using "I" or "We": Although using the first person ("I") can make your writing more personal, we have been advised by our reviewers, who just happen to be high school teachers (Don't worry, we've got you covered!), that it is best to stay away from that when writing essays in school. Unless you get a "What I Did on My Summer Vacation" sort of prompt that particularly asks about *your* life experience, it's best to keep yourself out of it.

Take a Picture

Huh? Isn't this a fourth catchy intro tip? We *appreciate* all the tips . . . we really do . . . but I think "*Buffy's*" on, and I *thought* this section was *so over* . . .

Sorry, bear with us a few more minutes. Yes, we did sneak in one more catchy intro tip, but there's a method to our madness! In fact, we don't recommend that most of you use this for writing you do in school—because this one is HARD! However, for those of you who actually like to write, have a *flair* for writing as they say, "taking a picture" is a pretty cool way of introducing your thoughts on a matter. This is more in line with *creative writing*, which we'll touch on in the last chapter of the book. So to those who just want to learn the basics for creating a fairly good essay, skip this! But if you *are* interested, please read on.

Imagine taking a photo of the situation you want to talk about, and then, instead of telling the reader your own thoughts, you simply *describe the picture*. If the picture is vivid enough, the reader will be able to *infer* what you mean to say without you actually saying it. How does that work? We're going to look at how Chi has responded to our original prompt, **"Should school start later in the day?"** by Taking a Picture (guess she didn't run out on us to watch *"Buffy"* after all!):

Morning light has broken. A shaft of light streams across the room, illuminating the face of a teenaged girl who lies fast asleep on her bed. Suddenly, there is a screeching sound that rips through her body like a torrential tide. The girl bolts upright in her bed, her eyes wide open. She turns to her alarm clock and sees the time: 7:00 A.M.! The girl's mouth opens, and a horrific shriek issues forth, joining the alarm clock to become one long, eerie note of despair.

Suddenly the door to her room flies open, and a woman calls out to the girl, "Come on now. Get up! You hear me? It's late, very late . . ."

The girl turns slowly around to her mother and stops screaming. But she continues to stare, her eyes blank, vacant, empty . . . like a zombie!

Oh-kay . . . Perhaps this may be a tad over the top, but although Chi has not stated how she feels, we get the same idea as we did before, which is that school starts too early (way too early in this case!), *and* it is having a very negative effect on teenagers. The message comes through loud and clear, and it's more fun to read! Again, the last chapter will go into this kind of writing.

Now it's time to get back to our essay. After all, we've only just finished the intro. We have four paragraphs to go! But, remember, now that we've done the intro, the rest is easy. So, let's get into our Supporting Paragraphs, or as we like to call them....

EASY PIECES 2, 3, AND 4—OR BING, BOING, AND BANG!

And so the second piece does the **bing**

and the third piece does the **boing**

and the fourth piece does the **bang**!

Cool!

Uh, yeah . . . really cool . . . kids, be afraid, be very afraid . . .

Well anyway, our 5 easy pieces, or our 5-paragraph plan,

requires you to write three supporting paragraphs, which are second, third, and fourth paragraphs in our plan. We're calling them the Bing, the Boing, and the Bang! If you think this is bad, you should know that some teachers call it the Bing, the Bang, and the Bongo! Now it's our turn to say . . . *WHATEVER*! In any case, it might sound kind of cheesy, and we don't know what teacher came up with which three words, but stay with us 'cause it works. Check it out:

* **Bing:** Your first supporting paragraph. It's your least powerful idea.

* **Boing:** Your second supporting paragraph. It's your next-to-most-important idea.

* **And Bang!:** As you may have guessed by now, your third supporting paragraph. This is, of course, your most important idea because you always want to *end* with your strongest idea.

We're hoping you remember something of Chapter 3, when we talked about paragraphs, but we'll just remind you of a few points:

* Write topic sentences for your supporting paragraphs. These are created from the points you raised in your thesis statement.

* Use specific examples and details. Make sure they relate to your topic sentence and don't wander off the subject.

* Move from one detail to the next with transitional words and phrases.

* Vary your sentence structure, and use concrete and interesting words so your reader won't fall asleep.

As we said, if the intro is done right, it will end with a strong thesis statement that will easily enable you to create your supporting paragraphs. But first let's look at what Bing, Boing, and Bang! really mean. It simply translates into the following:

* **Bing:** First reason to support your position.

* **Boing:** Second reason to support your position.

* **Bang!:** Third, and most important, reason to support your position.

Yep, that's all it is. So, let's look at Chi's intro again and find the Bing, the Boing, and the Bang!

School starts much too early in the morning. Kids keep falling asleep in class.**[BING]** The fact is their days and nights are so jam-packed with activities that they can't get to sleep at a decent hour.**[BOING]** It's totally abnormal, and it's turning them into zombies.**[BANG!]**!

Now we are going to create our topic sentences for second, third, and fourth paragraphs. How? We will simply *reword* Chi's thesis statement and plug it into bing, boing, and bang:

* One reason school should start later is so that kids don't fall asleep in class.

* Another reason is kids have so much to do that it is impossible to get to sleep early enough.

* The final reason is they are turning into vegetables who will have little to offer the future world in which they will live.

That was pretty easy, right? As you can see, we slightly revised what Chi said, but not by much. Note we emphasized Chi's idea that kids were turning into **zombies** for our third topic sentence, our bang!, by now saying they were turning into **vegetables**.

Now that we have our topic sentences, Chi's going to plug in the necessary ingredients we told you about (specific examples and transitional words) and create our supporting paragraphs. Here's the first:

To begin, [TRANSITION] kids are constantly falling asleep in class [TOPIC SENTENCE]. In class just the other morning, a teacher called on a student to answer a question. Of course, [TRANSITION] at the moment all the other students turned to look at her, she let out a loud snore! [SPECIFIC EXAMPLE]

You have to admit that was pretty painless. Note that Chi started with a transition (see page 65 of Chapter 3) so her topic sentence didn't appear out of nowhere, and she slightly reworded the first part of her thesis statement. By adding the word *constantly*, she was able to emphasize her topic sentence, and by providing an example, she illustrated how this was not a healthy or positive thing. Simple, clear, and to the point, right?

Now on to the second supporting paragraph. You do the exact thing except that in order to be a little bit stronger than the first paragraph, you need to use supporting details that the reader will find even more compelling:

Unfortunately, **[TRANSITION]** kids have so much to do that it is impossible to get to sleep early enough. **[TOPIC SENTENCE]** Teachers do not realize that all the other teachers are also giving homework, so as a result, kids can end up spending anywhere from 3 to 5 hours working their way through history, lit, algebra, and chemistry homework! **[SPECIFIC EXAMPLE]** Additionally, **[TRANSITION]** their parents have them taking piano and tennis lessons, not to mention the chores they give them, like walking the dog, picking up groceries from the store, setting and clearing the table, and cleaning their rooms. As a result, [TRANSITION] kids can't even start their homework until after 8! [ANOTHER SPECIFIC EXAMPLE] Therefore, [TRANSITION] they are often up to 1 in the morning completing all their tasks. That leaves them with less than 5 hours of sleep before the alarm clock rings, and they are up doing it all over again! [YET ANOTHER EXAMPLE]

By citing more examples, the paragraph sounds stronger than the first, but it also sounds different...not quite a Bing, maybe a Boing? Well, different in any case. By supplying two long lists (*algebra, history, lit*, etc., and *walking the dog, picking up groceries, setting the table*, etc.), Chi was also able to change the *pattern* of her sentence structure. So, her point is a little stronger and a little clearer. Great! On to the third supporting paragraph, the **Bang**!

(**Remember:** Do not worry about grammar or punctuation for now. We know about the mistakes!)

As we said, you need to save the strongest reason for last. But, once again, the same methods still apply:

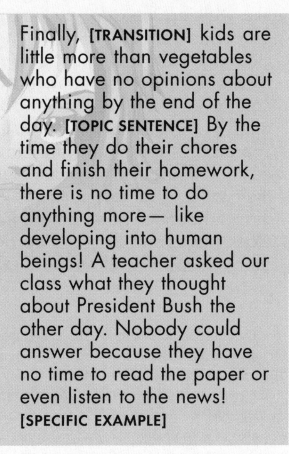

Finally, **[TRANSITION]** kids are little more than vegetables who have no opinions about anything by the end of the day. **[TOPIC SENTENCE]** By the time they do their chores and finish their homework, there is no time to do anything more— like developing into human beings! A teacher asked our class what they thought about President Bush the other day. Nobody could answer because they have no time to read the paper or even listen to the news! **[SPECIFIC EXAMPLE]**

That wasn't so hard. Again, Chi reworded the topic sentence and added more examples. Note that she saved her strongest examples for last. The fact that kids have no opinion about the president of our country is a pretty strong statement.

So, in a nutshell, what are we doing here? Basically, we are rewording the topic sentence, providing a few examples (taken from your brainstorming notes), and adding a few transitions. We did this three times (the Bing, the Boing, the Bang!). So, we're done, right? Except for one little pesky thing.

EASY PIECE 5: THE CONCLUSION

Oh, that thing . . . THE FINAL CONCLUSION! THE FINAL FRONTIER! THE LAST STATEMENT! THE KICKER! THE...

It's not so bad. Yes, you do have to wrap up your whole essay in a single paragraph, and you do have to be certain that your reader understands your position. And you also have to make your essay come full circle by restating your thesis. But it isn't a big deal. In the same way that you re-stated your topic sentences and turned them into supporting paragraphs, we'll do the same thing...with a few additional, **but easy**, steps. Check this out:

In conclusion, **[ENDING TRAN-SITION]** it is clearly essential to the future of this world that school start later in the day. **[RESTATING POSITION IN NEW WORDS]**

It is sad but true that [TRANSITION] kids all over America are falling asleep in class and turning into mindless beings who have no ideas about anything. If this situation continues, we face a dismal future and a country run by a group of people incapable of thinking about anything or caring about anyone.

Done! That was easy! Chi slightly reworded her position by making it bigger. Instead of just restating that school should start later in the day, she added that it was "essential to the future of this world."

Chi did something else as well. As you can see, she left the reader with a scary prediction of what the world will be like if school doesn't start later in the day.

The conclusion: This isn't the place to grovel—that means no "I hope you feel the same way as I do" or "Of course, everyone has his or her own opinion, and this is just what I think." Say it like you mean it, forcefully and confidently. Finally, try to give the reader something to think about. Whether it's an evaluation of the information you've presented, a recommendation of what you and/or the reader should do next, or a prediction of what the future holds for your subject, demonstrate that your subject made you think and that you hope it will make your reader think, too.

Here are our words of advice on your essay's big finale:

★ Don't contradict your thesis statement. If your position has changed by the time you reach the end of your essay, go back and rewrite the whole thing to reflect this change. Unfortunately, if you changed your position, you'll also have to write a new thesis statement, so our advice is: Don't do it! Stick to your position.

★ Don't introduce new information or details in the conclusion. Stay on the subject and only discuss what you've already proven or what directly relates to your thesis.

★ Don't apologize for not being an authority. Otherwise, your reader will ask, "Why did I bother reading this whole thing if the writer doesn't know what she's talking about?" No matter how limited your experience may be, you are an authority because no one else has the power to decide your opinions.

Uh . . . thought I'd say hi. Actually, the authors asked me to fill up some white space! Weird . . .

Get Wise!

Respond to the following prompt by writing an essay. As we had fun while learning how to build a well-constructed piece of writing, we are giving you a more "serious" prompt, which is more like something you would get in class. Remember to use your basic 5-paragraph plan and to include all the things we talked about in the last few chapters.

Prompt—Are Americans doing all they can to protect the environment?

How Wise?

Here's our essay to respond to the given prompt. Note we have called out all the required ingredients you learned about in the last few chapters.

Prompt—Are Americans doing all they can to protect the environment?

Americans have long understood the importance of protecting their environment. But are Americans taking the necessary steps to ensure that this occurs? **[ASK A QUESTION]** Unfortunately, the answer is no. They drive gas-guzzling cars. **[BING!]** The products they buy are sold in packaging that often cannot be recycled. **[BOING!]** And they waste water and spread toxic chemicals so our lawns are lush and green. **[BANG!]** They have done little to change their lifestyles, even though they know they are hurting the environment. **[THESIS STATEMENT]**

To begin with, **[TRANSITION]** Americans stubbornly refuse to change their transportation habits. **[BING!]** Unlike the Europeans and Japanese, Americans prefer to drive their own cars rather than take trains or buses. Look, for example, at Los Angeles, California. The freeways are backed up for two, sometimes three hours during rush hour as millions of people drive to work. All of these cars have contributed to an unhealthy cloud of smog as pollutants leave vehicle exhaust pipes and enter the air. Further, in recent years American-designed cars have grown larger and waste gasoline. American SUVs, which were originally designed to be driven off-road, rarely leave the highways. And the oversize luxury cars that are favored by retired Americans get terrible mileage. On the contrary, European and Japanese cars have become both more compact and more energy-efficient. The Swiss Smart car is about the same size as a golf cart, uses considerably less fuel, and is perfect for traveling around a city without releasing pollutants into the environment. Japanese manufacturers have brought cars to the market that use alternative sources of fuel. **[SUPPORTING SENTENCES]** Yet many Americans continue to drive vehicles that waste energy.

Second, **[TRANSITION]** many of the products Americans buy come with a lot of packaging that cannot be recycled. **[BOING!]** A few years ago, grocery stores began offering a discount to shoppers who used their own bags rather than using the new plastic bags at the checkout line. But the discount is so small—usually only a few pennies per bag—that most Americans do not find it worth the inconvenience to reuse bags. Instead, they bring home new plastic bags with each trip to the store. While Americans may use those bags to line our garbage cans, eventually they end up in the local landfill, where it takes decades for them to disintegrate. In addition, products like refrigerators, dishwashers, and exercise equipment are packed in large cardboard boxes and cushioned with Styrofoam "peanuts" to prevent damage. Although the boxes and peanuts are made from recycled paper and plastic, most people are unable to recycle them because most American towns usually limit recycling to plastic, glass, and newspapers. **[SUPPORTING SENTENCES]** As a result, they continue to send more trash to landfills than is necessary.

Finally, **[TRANSITION]** Americans use unnatural methods to keep their lawns and gardens lush. **[BANG!]** For example, keeping the grass green requires a great deal of water. As long as it rains, they leave things alone. But if a couple of days pass without showers and the grass begins to turn brown, they grab their garden hoses, hook up their sprinklers, and soak their lawns. Americans drain hundreds, even thousands, of gallons of water from our reservoirs each time they water the grass. Yet it would be more productive to save that water for farming, fire fighting, or even for drinking. Then, to make matters worse, Americans spread toxic pesticides in their yards to kill weeds and plant-eating insects. While this succeeds in destroying unwanted pests, it comes with significant risks. Scientists have discovered that the chemicals seep into the soil and eventually enter the drinking water. Further, the chemicals often kill more than just the pests. Harmless animals like butterflies and frogs become contaminated by pesticides that are either absorbed into the vegetation they eat or directly through their skin. **[SUPPORTING SENTENCES]** As a result of trying to keep their gardens pretty, Americans end up wasting a valuable resource and polluting the environment.

To conclude, **[TRANSITION]** Americans have little interest in protecting the environment. They drive large vehicles that pollute the environment. They put the products they buy in nonrecyclable packages. And they waste water and cover their lawns with toxic chemicals in order to make them green. **[RE-STATES INTRODUCTION IN NEW WORDS]** So far, Americans have been lucky. But some day they will run out of gasoline, their garbage dumps will overflow with trash, animals will disappear, and their water will be in short supply or completely unusable. Americans will be forced to change their attitude toward the environment, but by that time, it will be too late. The Earth will become uninhabitable. **[ENDING GIVES THE READER SOMETHING TO THINK ABOUT]**

chapter 6

Pop, Sparkle & Squeak

(or How to Edit Your Writing)

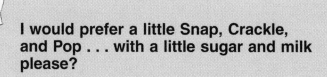

I would prefer a little Snap, Crackle, and Pop . . . with a little sugar and milk please?

123

Get Wise! Mastering Writing Skills   www.petersons.com

So what the heck is Pop, Sparkle & Squeak? Well, it is not a cereal, so if you're hungry, please come back to this chapter later! But if you're ready to start learning how to edit, then let's talk about editing!

Before we start, let's review what we've learned so far:

★ How to brainstorm and come up with a thesis statement

★ How to create topic sentences with examples to back them up in each of our paragraphs

★ How to create transitions so that our thoughts flow smoothly and the reader is able to follow your thoughts

★ How to create a "catchy" intro

★ How to create a conclusion that restates your thesis and ensures that the reader understands your position

★ How to create variety in your sentences so that the entire essay does not read as if it's been written by a member of the Borg or some robotic humanoid

Uh, sure . . . we may have learned all that but I'm not sure my essay contained *all* of those ingredients. I may have a big head but not big enough to remember all those things!

That's *OK! That's why we edit!* We guarantee you that even the most accomplished writers need to go back and rewrite, and rewrite again.

Editing reminds me of baseball. Batters get more than one chance to hit the ball, so why should writers have to get it right at the first swing?

We must be doing something right here. Chi not only made a cool analogy but more important there was no sarcasm in that remark!

Uh oh...What's happening to me?

Have you ever looked closely at the word *revision* and thought about what it really means?

Re-vision

When you break the word apart and look at each part separately, it means literally "seeing again." Now that you have crafted a well-structured essay, and you no longer have to worry about the hard part, like coming up with ideas, a thesis statement, and strong examples to back up your topic sentences, you can look more closely at your essay and make sure that it is perfect. In other words, "you can see it again" with new eyes. Which brings us to our chapter title: Pop, Sparkle & Squeak.

POP

This is about the big picture. This is not a point where you'll be thinking about technical details, like grammar. These are literally the things that will POP out at you if they are wrong.

The big things will also pop out at your teacher! As it is, she's probably going to tear her hair out, gouge her eyes out, and go running through the streets screaming, "The horror! The horror!" by the time she's read her twelfth incoherent essay.

So, how do you make sure there are no major pop-outs? It's easy. You know all this stuff, but it always makes it easier if you have a basic checklist in front of you.

Ask yourself the following questions:

★ Does the introduction "hook" the reader with an interesting lead, like making a prediction, asking a question, or challenging a commonly held belief? (See page 101)

★ Are there transitions between ideas? Does each paragraph logically follow the paragraph before it? (See page 65)

★ Word choice: Are the words appropriate to the piece of writing? Is the writing appropriately formal or informal? Are there any redundancies or useless words that can be cut? (See page 24)

It's good to have a list, right? Let's review Chi's essay from the previous chapter, and at the same time, let's look at our list and see how we can improve it:

School starts much too early in the morning. Kids keep falling asleep in class. The fact is their days and nights are so jampacked with activities that they can't get to sleep at a decent hour. It's totally abnormal, and it's turning them into zombies!

To begin, kids are constantly falling asleep in class. In class just the other morning, a teacher called on a student to answer a question. Of course, at the moment all the other students turned to look at her, she let out a loud snore!

Unfortunately, kids have so much to do that it is impossible to get to sleep early enough. Teachers do not realize that all the other teachers are also giving homework, so as a result, kids can end up spending anywhere from 3 to 5 hours working their way through history, lit, algebra, and chemistry home-work! Additionally, their parents have them taking piano and tennis lessons, not to mention the chores they give them, like walking the dog, picking up groceries from the store, setting and clearing the table, and cleaning their rooms. As a result, kids can't even start their homework until after 8! There-fore, they are often up to 1 in the morning completing all their tasks. That leaves them with less than 5 hours of sleep before the alarm clock rings, and they are up doing it all over again.

Finally, kids are little more than vegetables who have no opinions about anything by the end of the day. By the time they do their chores and finish their homework, there is no time to do anything more—like develop-ing into human beings! A teacher asked our class what they thought about President Bush the other day. Nobody could answer be-cause they have no time to read the paper or even listen to the news!

In conclusion, it is clearly essential to the future of this world that school start later in the day. It is sad but true that kids all over America are falling asleep in class and turn-ing into mindless beings who have no ideas about anything. If this situation continues, we face a dismal future and a country run by a group of people incapable of thinking about anything or caring about anyone.

Let's start off with the introduction. We know that Chi has created a thesis statement and that she has correctly followed that up with related topic sentences and examples in the following paragraphs. The introduction is strong because she makes a prediction (". . . it's turning them into zombies.") But what pops out at you in this first paragraph?

Hmmm. Now that I think of it, I guess any talk about zombies is not going to go over well in school . . .

Chi is correct. In Chapter 2, we talked about tone and using appropriate words (see page 33). If you look back at our Pop list, you'll see that you do need to think about your audience and whether your word choice is correct.

Is the word *zombies* really in keeping with this kind of essay? Back in Chapter 2, we also talked about keeping a thesaurus and dictionary at your side. What other words could you use that would have the same meaning as *zombie*, and yet still get Chi's point across strongly? Here are some alternate words from a thesaurus:

automaton

robot

android

Unfortunately, we don't think any of these work well because the tone is still wrong. All of these words are similar to *zombie*. Remember, the tone needs to be appropriate to what you are writing about. If you were writing a science-fiction or horror story, any of these words could work. But, this is an essay for school.

 **A better, more appropriate word for z*ombie?* How about my fifth-period study hall monitor? Or, there's always that lunch room monitor. She would fill the bill just fine!**

If none of the words work, you can use the dictionary or the thesaurus *again*! That's right, and look up the *second* set of words. Then you'll get more choices. Here's what we got:

machine

That's not bad. What else pops out at you and seems inappropriate now that we've gotten rid of the zombie? Here's what Chi found. Take a look at the handwritten edits and see if you agree with the changes.

School starts much too early in the morning. ~~Kids~~ _Students_

keep falling asleep in class. ~~The fact is~~ T̂heir days

and nights are so jam-packed with activities that

they can't get to sleep at a decent hour. ~~It's totally~~

In addition, students have little chance to do anything
other than schoolwork.

~~abnormal, and it's turning them into zombies!~~

As a result, modern-day students are becoming more like
machines rather than developing into full-rounded people.

So, how exactly has Chi revised her work? Again, what popped out and what changed as a result?

★ "Kids" seemed as inappropriate as "zombies." "Kids" was changed to "students."

★ "The fact is" is a redundancy. These are unnecessary words. Note that without these words the meaning is exactly the same. This was deleted.

As you may also see, the word _machines_ did not fit neatly into Chi's final statement. She couldn't just replace _zombies_ with _machines_. However, it made her stop and "see again" what she did say and whether or not it was a fully formed thought.

In rethinking the zombie sentence, she had the chance to see that she hadn't really explained herself. Chi had made a jump from the fact that students had a lot of activities to the fact that they were turning into machines. Something else is needed to make that point clear, and that "something else" is that kids aren't developing into well-rounded people. Once you have the basic gist of what you want to say down on paper, you can then look carefully at everything you've written and make sure it is crystal clear.

Note that by adding one particular sentence ("In addition, students have little chance to do anything other than schoolwork"), the whole paragraph starts to change. Chi thinks school should start later, but we also understand why she thinks students are turning into machines—because they have little time for anything else but school!

Chi obviously checked her list a few times. Other than deleting the inappropriate words, she also noticed a transition was needed at the end of her intro. Then her final thoughts about students turning into machines flowed easily from the previous sentence. Instead of just making the statement bluntly, a little add-on, such as *As a result*, creates a kind of hook, leading the reader into her final intro statement. Also, she more fully explained her thoughts about students turning into machines.

If any of your words sound like they just dropped by like an unwanted guest . . . or if they sound like a sudden thud . . . you probably need a transition!

SPARKLE

Sparkle, unlike Pop, does not pop out at you. This part of the editing process is a bit more subtle, more like when Chi rewrote the last part of her intro statement because it wasn't quite clear. It's taking OK writing and turning it into really good writing that is strong and fully developed. It's the difference between wiping your floors clean so they shine or waxing them so they sparkle . . .

When the authors start talking about floor cleaners, that's your first hint that it's been a long time since high school . . . or college . . . or anything for them. Kind of scary that we've been spending this much time with them, isn't it?

On that note, we'll forget the analogies and just move on to giving you our Sparkle list:

* Does each body paragraph talk about your main point, or does it get off the subject?

* Are the paragraphs balanced? Are there any that are too short? Or too long?

* Is there any place where the argument is weak? Does each detail present new information to further support your Thesis statement?

* Does your conclusion restate or summarize the main point of your essay and effectively end the essay, leaving the reader with a clear idea of your position?

Reread the second paragraph carefully. Does it sound right? Or does something seem to be missing? Let's look at Chi's notes on the second paragraph:

To begin, ~~kids~~ ^{students} are constantly falling asleep in class. ~~In~~

~~class~~ just the other morning, a teacher called on a

student to answer a question. Of course, at ~~the~~ ^{that} mo-

ment all the other students turned to look ~~at her,~~ she let ^{because the student}

out a loud snore! (Too short!)

Note that first Chi used her Pop list and changed the obvious problems that we already discussed:

★ "Kids" to "students"

★ Deleting "In class," which is redundant as she already indicated the students were in class

★ Adding "because" for transition and smooth flow

On close examination, however, it becomes clear that the second paragraph is not quite finished. Although Chi gave an example of how students are falling asleep in class, she didn't provide enough detail. Remember, the purpose of providing detail is to support your thesis statement.

Look at the second and third points on our Sparkle list. Even if you weren't able to figure out that something was wrong with this paragraph, you can use this list to recheck yourself. The second item asks if the paragraphs are balanced and if any are a lot shorter or longer than the rest.

You can see clearly that the second paragraph is a lot shorter than the rest. This could be a sign that something is wrong. Read the next item. It asks if every detail presents a *new* piece of information.

Although Chi presents the detail of a student snoring in class, has any new information really been provided? Do you, as the reader, know anything more than you knew from the first paragraph? The answer is no. We already knew from the introductory paragraph that kids were falling asleep in class.

Our Sparkle list alerts us to two red flags that something is wrong:

* The paragraph is much shorter than the rest of the paragraphs.

* We have not learned anything new.

Here's how Chi revised the second paragraph to include new information:

To begin, students are constantly falling asleep in class. Just the other morning, a teacher called on a student to answer a question. Of course, at that moment, all the students turned to look because the student let out a loud snore! The student was so humiliated when all the other students turned and laughed that she could barely concentrate. The rest of the class could not concentrate either. They were either sleeping themselves or busy laughing at the snoring event. In any case, whether students are sleeping in class or watching others sleeping in class, it doesn't seem that any of them are actually paying attention to the teacher and learning anything.

By adding new information, the paragraph has grown in size. But also, now it explains how getting up so early is not only a problem for students who are tired but also for the students who are *affected* by the sleeping students. Nobody is concentrating on what the teacher is teaching! They are either too tired or watching the sleepers.

Again, this does not pop out at you immediately. You have to read and think about what you are saying. If you want to write a strong essay that sparkles, check out the above list and reread what you've written. While you may have all the basic facts down on paper, it may be necessary to further elaborate by presenting new details that provide new information and more fully support your thesis statement. A short paragraph isn't *always* a problem. In some cases, it is possible to present details in a clear, succinct way. Sometimes one example can be so strong it may not be necessary to elaborate. But, remember, you are not going to convince your reader of anything by *repeating* the same facts in a different way or in another paragraph. Most important is whether or not each of the supporting paragraphs provides *new* information. So, if a supporting paragraph seems short, check again for *new* details.

A first draft that escapes the editing process without many changes was written either by a genius or by someone who doesn't want to sound like a genius.

Using the Pop and Sparkle lists, here is how Chi has edited the rest of her essay:

students

Unfortunately, ~~kids~~ have so much to do that it is

impossible to get to sleep early enough. Teachers do

(italics)

not realize that all the _other_ teachers are _also_ giving

students

homework, so ~~as a result,~~ ~~kids~~ end up spending any-

where from 3 to 5 hours working their way through

history, lit, algebra, and chemistry homework! ~~Addi-~~

And between after-school

~~tionally, their parents have them taking~~ piano ~~and ten-~~

basketball practice, and

nis lessons, ~~not to mention the~~ chores ~~they give them,~~

~~like walking the dog, picking up groceries from the~~

~~store, setting and clearing the table, and cleaning their~~

run-on sentence?

used
"as a result"
in intro

students don't
rooms. ~~As a result, kids can't~~ even start their home-

This means
work until after 8! ~~Therefore~~, they are often up to 1 in

the morning completing all their tasks. That leaves them

with less than 5 hours of sleep before the alarm clock

rings, and they are up doing it all over again!

students
Finally, ~~kids~~ are little more than vegetables who

have no opinions about anything by the end of the

day. By the time they do their chores and finish their

homework, there is no time to do anything else—like

For example, a
developing into human beings! ~~A~~ teacher asked our

class what they thought about President Bush the other

day. Nobody could answer because they have no time

to read the paper or even listen to the news!

In conclusion, it is clearly essential to the future of this world that school start later in the day. It is sad but true that kids all over America are falling asleep in class and turning into mindless beings who have no ideas about anything. If this situation continues, we face a dismal future and a country run by a group of people incapable of thinking about anything or caring about anyone.

As you can see, many of the problems were similar to what Chi found in the first two paragraphs. This is often the case. People tend to repeat the same errors.

But, note on page 137 that Chi is worried about what she fears may be a run-on sentence. In fact, it *is* a run-on sentence. Sometimes—but not always— a run-on sentence can work for two reasons. (1) The length of the sentence might contribute to the point you are trying to make (in this case, kids have so much to do after school, so you want to leave the reader breathless, too.) (2) On pages 44–51 we talked about varying sentence lengths and creating rhythm in your writing. However, when Chi re-read her essay, she decided this sentence ran on for so long that she would lose her reader's attention—and you *never* want that to happen!

Look at the last Sparkle bullet. Remember, this is the *closing* paragraph. It is your way of saying goodbye. Once you've restated your thesis statement in new words, as Chi has done here, the final line should send the reader off on his or her merry way. Therefore, Chi has moved her "In conclusion" line to the very end.

Try reading the closing paragraph both ways. As you can see, the first way sort of leaves the reader in the middle of a thought. But by moving a phrase such as "In conclusion" to the end, the reader is left with a sense of completion. It's like adding "The End" to the end of a story or a period at the end of a sentence. It is a signal to readers that they have reached a close to the argument. "In conclusion" is a standard windup, and it is fine to use if you can't think of anything else.

SQUEAK

The last step in the writing process is about being "Squeaky Clean." Now you get to proofread your words and sentences for errors—mainly grammatical errors—so your writing is at its very best.

Editing for grammatical errors sounds like my last check in the mirror, and suddenly I'm there for another 20 minutes tucking in my shirt or smoothing down that piece of hair that's sticking up and making me look like a total geek!

This is a great analogy. Writing is similar to dressing up nicely. It doesn't matter whether you are wearing a silk shirt and the latest designer jeans. If something's out of whack, like you're wearing soccer cleats with a prom dress or a tux, it can upset the whole picture.

Of course, the total exception is when you want your designer jeans to have a ripped-up hole in the middle of the knee, in which case that completes the look!

When you check your writing for grammatical errors, you are going to be looking for things like:

* Sentence fragments

* Comma splices

* Run-on sentences

* Subject and verb agreement

★ Misplaced modifiers

Those pesky modifiers! They're always getting lost. Maybe you can find them in the same place that all those lost socks go!

★ Double negatives

I don't never use no double negatives. No, not me!

We're not going to spend too much time on grammar because if your skills are not up to par, we can't help you in just a few small paragraphs. If you need grammar help, there are a lot of great books that can really make a world of difference to your writing. Of course, there's *Get Wise! Mastering Grammar Skills*. Another great little book (it really *is* a tiny book) that covers almost all you need to know is Strunk and White's *The Elements of Style*.

Again, read and study the above books if you feel you need some real help in the grammar department. Otherwise, on the following page we give you a little section called *Grammar Glamour*. This is a list of common grammatical errors that students often make and some quick tricks to overcome these mistakes.

Note the little dashes on the side of the pages. If you'd like, you can cut this section out and carry it with you as a little reference guide.

GRAMMAR GLAMOUR

The following list contains common grammatical errors. Again, this is a quick reference guide to errors. Think of it as your personal arsenal to combat bad grammar. These mistakes are so common that you're bound to hear people make them every day. Many of the items involve word confusion. When the following words are used incorrectly, they can drastically alter the meaning of a sentence.

Affect / Effect

This confuses many people. **Affect** means to *influence* something.

> The fashion on the runways **affects** the fashions in lower-priced stores.

Effect is the *result* of something.

> The fashion shown on the runways has an inspiring **effect** on me.

So, something **affects** you, and you are **effected** by it.

Accept / Except

Another thing people get confused about. **Accept** means *to approve of, to welcome.*

> When I was finally **accepted** by the cool kids, I realized they were idiots.

Except means the same thing as *but*.

> I would have been happy to have finally been
> **accepted** by the cool kids, **except** I realized that
> they were idiots.

A lot

A lot is not one word. The phrase is two words and it means "plenty." It is a good idea to avoid using this phrase in formal writing. If you do use it, don't use it as follows: *alot.*

> There are **a lot** of cranky kids reading this
> writing book.

Already / All ready

Already is an adverb that tells when. **All ready** is a phrase meaning "completely ready."

> We are **already** on Chapter 6. We are **all ready**
> to stop studying our writing skills and play some
> video games!

Can / May

Can means **"able to"** and **may** means **"permitted to."**

I think we **can** finish studying writing skills. **May** we go now?

Imply / Infer

Something is **implied**. Someone **infers**. That is, you can say something that **implies** something to someone, and they **infer** what you mean.

I **implied** that Shelly is not my favorite person. Angela somehow **inferred** from this that I absolutely hate Shelly.

Its / It's

Only use **it's** when you mean "**it is**."

It's snowing outside.

There is no other time when you need an apostrophe in "**its**." Even when **its** is possessive, it still gets no apostrophe. **It's** is only correct when you are saying **it is**. We can't seem to say this enough, as we keep repeating ourselves.

Lay / Lie

Lay means to "to place." **Lie** means "to recline."

Please **lay** your cup upon the table. When you are done, you may **lie** down and rest upon our big comfy couch.

Sympathy / Empathy

To have **sympathy** for someone else means to feel bad about that person's situation, which *you have never experienced.*

I have **sympathy** for the starving children of the world.

To experience **empathy** means you feel bad about someone's situation, and you *have experienced the same thing.*

I really **empathize** with Emily; I swallowed a bug once, too.

There / Their / They're

Tricky, huh? No, easy. Use **there** for location.

The party is over **there**.

Their is a pronoun, and it is the possessive form of **they**. Only use it when referring to something that belongs to "them."

Their dog is adorable. (The dog *belongs* to them.)

They're is a *contraction* of the words *they* and *are*. Only use *they're* if you mean **they are.**

They're coming over for dinner tonight.

They

Lots of people seem to forget that **they** is a plural pronoun and will mix it with a singular noun or pronoun in a sentence.

INCORRECT: Someone started a nasty rumor about Amy, and then **they** started one about Sara.

This is incorrect. **They** is plural and **someone** is singular. In this kind of sentence, you must use **he** or **she** and not **they.** If you don't know the gender of the "someone," choose either **he** or **she** or use **he/she** if you must.

CORRECT: Someone started a nasty rumor about Amy, and then **he** started one about Sara.

To / Two / Too

Most, but not all, people use **two** correctly; that is, for the number 2. But **to** and **too** cause a lot of problems.

To is a preposition. Use it that way.

I went **to** the pep rally.

Too means *also.* Do not use it for location. And don't use it at the beginning of a sentence. You will often see **too** at the end of a sentence—don't forget the comma before **too**.

I went **to** the pep rally, and Janna had to go, **too**.

Who / Whom

We would bet that 99 percent of the population gets this wrong. It's a tough one, but we have a trick! First, however, we'll explain it so you understand the grammatical reasoning behind it (We have to do that, of course!): **Who** is used as the *subject* of the sentence. **Whom** is used as a direct *object*. Get it? Forget it! Here's the trick: There are two times when you use **whom**.

1. When a subject or a subject pronoun follows your choice of *who* or *whom*, use **whom.** Check this out:

It was the new baby-sitter_____ Lisa told to order that pizza!

Whom or who? The answer is **whom**. "Lisa" comes *after* your choice.

It was the new baby-sitter _____ordered that pizza.

Whom or who? The answer is **who**. There is no other subject following the choice. Therefore, **who** is the subject and follows the rule of being used as subject! Let's try it again, so you can get this right and correct your parents, teachers, and anyone older than you **whom** you think should know more than you, right? There we go! "You" followed the choice of *who* or *whom*, so you use **whom.** Cool trick, right? There's one little problem. There's an exception. You cannot use **whom** with the verb *to be*. That means if you see *is, are, was, were,* etc., stick with **who**. Sorry. Nothing is ever that simple. So, if your sentence reads:

You are the one ___ I love.

Who or whom? The answer is **who**. Since you see a form of the verb *to be*, in this case, *are*, use **who.**

2.   If a preposition comes before the choice, use **whom** since it will then become an object.

My mom asked, "The pizza was ordered by **whom?**"

Here's another *who/whom* trick: When in doubt, use **who**. Why? As we said, most people really can't get this right. And, **whom** used incorrectly sounds a lot worse than **who**. However, it would be great to get this right. So, read through this *who/whom* deal one more time. The thing is that once you get it, you'll never forget it, and you'll always get it right!

Which / That

This one is worse than *who* and *whom*. Again, few people get this right. And, of course, we have another tip for you! Think of it like this: The word *which* has the letter *c* in it. Think *c* for comma. It is almost always the case that a comma will come before your choice of **which.**

I am wearing this weird shirt, ____ is blue with purple blobs, but it will have to do.

Which or that? The answer is **which.** Note the comma that comes before the choice of *which* or *that.* Also, you can delete the phrase *which is blue with purple blobs* and the sentence will still make sense. *Which* is used as a connector for a phrase that is parenthetical to the core sentence. In other words, if you can delete the phrase that begins with *which* or *that,* and the sentence still makes sense on its own, use *which.* Can you do that?

I am wearing this weird shirt, but it will have to do.

The answer is yes. Of course, then, if no comma comes before your choice of *which* or *that,* you use **that:**

There is a statue ____ weighs more than 200 tons.

Which or that? The answer is **that.** No comma, and if you were to delete the phrase *that weighs more than 200 tons,* the sentence is left hanging: *There is a statue.* And? The phrase is necessary to the sentence, not parenthetical. As we said, this is a tough one. You could probably look through published books and find *which* and *that* used incorrectly. So, also read through this one again. It is very impressive to get this right, and all you really have to re-member is the letter *c*!

Your / You're

Your is a possessive pronoun. **You're** is a contraction for "you are."

> Where are **your** purple sneakers? **You're** making a fashion statement with those purple sneakers!

SOME ADDITIONAL ANNOYING DETAILS

In order to be absolutely squeaky clean, there's just one more thing to check other than grammatical accuracy: your handwriting! You need to make sure your handwriting is neat and legible. Just because *you* can read your handwriting doesn't mean anyone else can—nor should your reader be expected to puzzle over whether you've written *student* or *sident* (no, that's not a word!). Cross out any truly illegible words and neatly write above them in print. In fact, if you've got really bad handwriting, you should probably print your whole essay instead of using script.

Also check for misspelled words. The spell-check feature on most word-processing software will do this automatically for you, but there's always the chance that you might have used a homonym ("their" instead of "there" or "see" instead of "sea"). Watch for typos like extra periods and transposed letters ("form" instead of "from"). Make sure you've italicized or underlined titles of books, movies, and magazines. Check any quoted material in your essay against the original source; the last thing you need is to discover you've accidentally skipped a few words or lines or that you've referenced the wrong page or author. (You never know when your teacher might get an evil urge to look up the material for herself!)

Unless you've miraculously managed to write a perfect essay on the first draft, your paper is going to be a mess. Insert all of your edits (if you handwrote your essay, now is the time to type it on the computer) and print out a clean copy. Then check the new draft against your old draft to make sure you didn't miss any edits, and repeat the whole editing process at least one more time (unless you're working on a timed essay—you probably won't have time for more than one quick edit).

Yikes! Gulp! and EEk!

(or How to Write a Timed Essay)

The timed essay? This is almost as bad as that wonderful moment in life when you walk into class and your evil teacher decides to give you a **SURPRISE QUIZ!** Yuck! Even we authors still have nightmares about these high school moments! It's awful, and timed essays are almost as bad. But teachers love to give them for midterms, and they're required on a lot of standardized exams (notably the SAT II: Writing Test and a bunch of the APs).

153

Get Wise! Mastering Writing Skills   *www.petersons.com*

Yeah, timed essays are great moments for kids to remember! I'd take a Kodak moment any day over one of these!

We remember those moments well, and that's why we've devoted an entire chapter to the timed essay. In the same way that we gave you a 5-paragraph plan, we are going to give you a 4-step plan where we take you minute by minute through the timed essay so you never have to worry about this again.

What is a timed essay anyway? What does it look for? The timed essay doesn't just measure your knowledge of a subject, it also looks at your ability to respond to an argument, to organize your thoughts, and, oh yeah, to write coherently. All of that pressure hardly seems fair, especially when you've probably only got 45 minutes to write about a topic you've probably never thought about before and your only tools are a "blue book," a pen, and your brain.

For starters, no one expects you to write a mind-blowing essay in less than an hour. There just isn't time to come up with a revolutionary idea for ending racism or hunger or AIDS or illiteracy. Your teacher is primarily interested in whether you've understood the material that she covered in class and that you can write about it confidently. The person who grades your standardized test essay only cares about the mechanics of your writing.

Whomever ends up grading your essay is going to be looking for four things:

- ★ **Your thesis is fully developed.** Did you state your thesis clearly and support it with evidence in the body of the essay? Did you understand your topic, or does it sound like you had no idea what you were writing about?

- ★ **Your essay is organized.** Does it have an introduction? Are paragraphs that support your thesis arranged in a logical order? Is there a conclusion?

- ★ **Your essay focuses on the essay prompt.** Or did you wander around, get off track, and end up someplace that has nothing to do with what was originally asked?

- ★ **Your essay has been carefully edited.** Is it littered with spelling, punctuation, and grammar errors?

Seem similar to what we've already learned in the last six chapters? It is! Except that you have to do it in 45 minutes.

TACKLING THE TIMED ESSAY

Every second counts when you're faced with a device of academic torture as heinous and cruel as the timed essay test. Confront it with a solid plan of time management and a wristwatch.

We're going to assume you've got a total of 45 minutes to think about, write, and edit your essay. Place your watch on your desk and check it regularly to make sure you haven't fallen behind.

Minute 1

Read the essay prompt carefully. Nothing will kill your final grade faster than misunderstanding the question, and in a crunch situation like a timed essay, your brain can play all sorts of weird tricks on you. The last thing you want to do is write about "selling" boats when you're asked to write about "sailing" boats! Then try restating the prompt.

For our essay, we need to respond to the following prompt:

PROMPT—Defend or refute the following statement: E-mail's greatest strength—speed—is also its Achilles' heel.
(from Anne Fadiman's essay, "Mail")

Even if you don't know what an Achilles' heel is, you can figure out from the phrase "also" that the sentence sets up two opposing ideas. What's the opposite of "greatest strength"? "Greatest weakness" works—and it just so happens that's what an Achilles' heel is. But let's just assume

---

for a minute that you couldn't figure it out from the context clues; you've got no choice but to raise your hand and ask your teacher or the proctor for a quick definition.

Better to be embarrassed now than to flunk the test later because you didn't know what you were supposed to be writing about!

Sometimes an essay prompt will be a two- or three-part question:

Define the term "hip hop." Discuss three areas of American culture where hip hop plays a significant role, and explain how hip hop has crossed cultural barriers.

If you only write about *two* areas in American culture or if you forget to discuss how hip hop crossed over cultural barriers, your reader will have to knock down your score by a bunch of points because you haven't fully addressed the essay prompt. Make a list of all of the elements you need to answer and keep it by your side when you move on to the next step.

Minutes 2 through 6

Spend 4 minutes brainstorming your topic. Decide where you stand on the issue and draft a brief thesis statement: "Speed is e-mail's greatest weakness." You won't be allowed

continued on page 160

TICK TICK TICK TICK TICK TICK . . . .

Speed is e-mai
(The:

Time zones don't matter

Jokes written by others

Emoticons :-)
E-acronyms ROTFL

Lacks personality

No proofreading

Misspellings

Delete messages once we read them

Rarely save and store them

Europe to America in 3 seconds

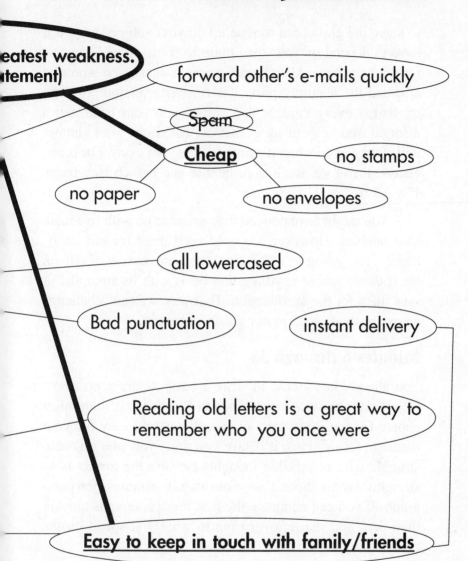

eatest weakness.
atement)

forward other's e-mails quickly

~~Spam~~

Cheap

no stamps

no paper

no envelopes

all lowercased

Bad punctuation

instant delivery

Reading old letters is a great way to remember who you once were

Easy to keep in touch with family/friends

to leave the classroom to read up on your subject, so you'll have to depend on your own brain to come up with support for your position. Also, because time is short, you won't be afforded the leisurely pace of a freewrite session. You can try listing every thought that comes into your head, but a disorganized heap of ideas that are listed one after another will slow you up when it's time to plan your essay. For timed essays, therefore, we like to bubble and branch (see pages 158–159).

You might have noticed that we came up with five main idea bubbles. However, we only need three for our essay. Since we're going to write about the weaknessess of e-mail, we'll either ignore anything that deals with its strengths or save them for the introduction. That way, we can "challenge an established idea" in our thesis statement.

Minutes 6 through 38

You already know how to write a basic 5-paragraph essay, so just practice what you learned in Chapter 5. It's the safest choice for the essay test: simple, direct, and easy for your reader to follow. Plus, it'll save you time; you won't have to struggle with connecting thoughts because the format is so straightforward. Spend no more than 6 minutes per paragraph. If you can complete the first four paragraphs quicker than that, add the leftover time to what you spend on the conclusion.

There isn't time to come up with a catchy introduction, so with your first sentence, just jump into your thesis statement. In the best of scenarios, an intelligent and engaging expression of your position will pop into your head.

While e-mail has improved the speed at which we communicate, that same speed has also caused the quality of our communication to deteriorate.

In a worst-case scenario—like nothing of interest occurs to you—*just restate the essay prompt* in a way that expresses your position.

Speed is e-mail's greatest strength, but it is also its greatest weakness.

You already know what to do with the supporting paragraphs, so we'll just remind you to stick with your main and supporting bubbles. Don't get off track, don't wander off into side conversations, and don't forget that everything you write must serve one purpose—to support your position.

Your conclusion is probably the most important element of a timed essay. It's the last thing your reader will remember, so you need to do more than summarize your position. Explain why your position is important or what kind of effects your solution might have. Try to pace yourself while you're writing the rest of the essay so you'll have a few extra minutes to work on your conclusion.

It's always better to end with a bang, not with a whimper, especially when your reader has a bunch of essays to plow through, she's got a headache, and her stomach is grumbling because she forgot to eat lunch!

Here's what we came up with for a conclusion to our essay:

> Although e-mail has enabled us to communicate with one another quickly, it has also caused our communication skills to deteriorate. E-mail is a cheap and fast substitute for the amount of time it takes to craft and mail a letter. A letter expresses the writer's personality, conveys information that is actually of interest to the writer and reader, follows the rules of writing, and can be saved and read over again for years to come. While e-mail certainly is cheap and fast, allowing us to increase the quantity of our communications with people far and wide, it also destroys the quality of what we say in those communications. In the long run, both readers and writers suffer for it.

A short statement, such as "readers and writers suffer for it," adds a nice kick to your essay and (hopefully) leaves your reader thinking.

A Few Notes on Writing

We've said this to you before but if you've got really bad handwriting—sloppy, tiny, disheveled—don't even bother writing in script. Printing is a lot slower and tedious, but you've got to remember your reader the whole time you're writing. If she can't read your essay because it's a mess, she's going to mark you down.

TICK TICK TICK TICK TICK TICK . . . .

But if you make things easy for your reader, she'll go easier on you when it's time to give you a grade. Another way to score brownie points is to leave room in the margins and double-space your essay. That way, you'll have plenty of room to insert your edits. Otherwise, your paper will be covered with little lines, arrows, and words written upside-down and squished in between other words.

One other thing to keep in mind: You won't be expected to quote from secondary sources unless they're provided to you, like on the AP U.S. History exam. Of course, if your essay exam is on something you've been studying in English class, like *Hamlet*, your teacher will be impressed if you throw a "To be or not to be" in your essay. A few well-chosen quotations demonstrate that you actually absorbed something from your class, but only when they actually fit your essay. Quoting for quoting's sake is never a good idea. And most important, make sure you get the quote right. Nothing will subtract points faster from your essay than a quote that's quoted wrong, especially if it's as famous as "to be or not to be." Imagine if you were reading a student essay that read "To be or not to be, That is the *answer*." The correct quote reads "That is the *question*." Like the students who were laughing at the snoring student in Chi's essay, that's all your teacher will be thinking about! So, unless you really remember the quote accurately, stay away from quoting, period!

Minutes 39 through 45

Time's almost up! Give the essay a quick read. Cross out and rewrite any handwriting that isn't legible, catch as many grammatical errors as you can, and make sure you haven't gotten off track with any rambling discussions that have nothing to do with your thesis statement.

TICK TICK TICK TICK TICK TICK . . . .

And make sure you haven't misspelled anything. Spell-check is a great tool for word-processing programs, but it's kind of hard to run it on a handwritten essay!

Punch up your intro and conclusion before the teacher or proctor calls "Pens down!" But don't waste time rewriting whole paragraphs. If you paid attention to your bubble chart, there shouldn't be any reason for a rewrite.

THE FINAL ESSAY

Thanks to e-mail, it is significantly easier to keep in touch with family and friends who live far away today than it was just a few years ago. We no longer have to worry about the physical distance that a letter must travel to reach its recipient. Even though the sender might live in New Jersey and the recipient might live in Switzerland, an e-mail can be sent and received in just a few seconds as opposed to the two weeks it often takes for a regular letter to travel. However, while e-mail has certainly improved the speed at which we communicate, that same speed has also caused a breakdown in the quality of our communication. E-mails lack the personality of a real letter, they are often riddled with grammatical errors, and they are rarely saved.

To begin with, because e-mails are so easily and quickly sent, writers do not take the time to infuse their messages with a sense of personality. Instead of expressing feelings and emotions in e-mail, we type generic "emoticons" like :-) when we're happy and acronyms like ROTFL (rolling on the floor laughing) when we find something amusing. Often, we do not even send our own original thoughts to our friends; instead, we forward someone else's joke, which probably passed through fifteen or twenty other computers before it reached us, or we cut and paste links to Web sites.

The writer of a real letter is limited in the amount of paper he can squeeze into an envelope, so he takes care to only include information that he thinks is important and that he knows will be of interest to his reader. On the contrary, the quality of most of the material that is sent via e-mail is little more than silly jokes passed from one e-mail user to another, regardless of whether the sender is interested in it or whether he thinks his recipient will care.

The speed with which an e-mail is delivered also has a significant affect on the speed with which we compose an e-mail. Besides the emoticons and acronyms that are peppered throughout our messages, we forget the basic rules of grammar and spelling. It is a rare person who runs a spell-check on his e-mail before mailing it, and it is an even rarer person who fully proofreads a message before clicking "Send." E-mails are constantly riddled with misspelled words, grammatical errors, and poor punctuation. Another side effect of how we compose a message is the use of capitalization. Some writers never bother capitalizing anything, so entire messages look like an e e cummings poem, while other writers leave the Caps Lock key on the whole time. While capitalization, grammar, and spelling might seem like minor problems, they detract from the recipient's reading experience as well as cast a poor light on the writer's ability to communicate with other people.

Finally, one of the joys of a traditional letter is being able to read it over and over again. Twenty years from now, you can still open a yellowed envelope and visit the thoughts of an old friend when she was young. But the speed of e-mail encourages us to delete our electronic messages once we have read them. E-mails do not exist in a physical format (unless we take the time to print them out) but in a series of binary codes that are projected as pixels onto a monitor. As a result, we place less importance on their existence than we would on a traditional letter. The recipient can destroy an e-mail just as easily as he or she opened it: with the simple click of a mouse. On occasion, a funny joke might be moved to the Saved Items box, but since we get with so many e-mails in a single day, the majority of messages are sent to the Trash box and forgotten.

Although e-mail has enabled us to communicate with one another quickly, it has also caused our communication skills to deteriorate. E-mail is a cheap and fast substitute for the amount of time it takes to craft and mail a letter. A letter expresses the writer's personality, conveys information that is actually of interest to the writer and reader, follows the rules of writing, and can be saved and read over again for years to come. While e-mail certainly is cheap and fast, allowing us to increase the quantity of our communications with people far and wide, it also destroys the quality of what we say in those communications. In the long run, both readers and writers suffer.

Get Wise!

The best way to get good at writing timed essays is to practice writing them. So, on the next few pages are a few prompts for you to try. Keep a timeclock or a wristwatch next to you and make sure you spend no more than 45 minutes on each essay. Use our 4-step plan and make sure you follow it. When you're done, ask a friend or your mom or dad to look it over and give you his or her opinion.

PROMPT—Should everyone in your high school
be required to have flu shots?

PROMPT—What is your position on dress codes for your high school?

PROMPT—Should school administrators be allowed to check student lockers?

SAMPLE ESSAYS

We have provided seven essays here. In each essay, we have called out the following important ingredients that ensure a well-crafted essay has been written:

* ★ Catchy Intro Technique
* ★ Thesis Statement
* ★ Topic Sentences (*Bing, Boing, Bang!*)
* ★ Transitions
* ★ Conclusion

179

Get Wise! Mastering Writing Skills   *www.petersons.com*

Of course, Chi has written two of the following seven essays. We're sure you will be able to figure out which ones they are.

Please note that while these are well-constructed essays, some have been written in fun. Chi, for example, obviously does not believe that Michael Jackson or Mariah Carey are aliens (or does she?) Nor does she think that Big Bird or Martha Stewart could be real characters on "The Real World." These are humorous essays for your entertainment only. However, she does use everything we've learned in this book to craft a good essay with strong supporting details all the way through. Most of your teachers will expect you to be serious when you write. So, while you may use these for reference in writing essays, we don't advise that you try to imitate Chi's particular style when you write in class. We cannot guarantee that your teacher will be amused!

1. PROMPT—Have extraterrestrials visited Earth?

Most people are convinced that aliens from outer space have never visited our planet. They use three reasons to support their position. First, there is no physical evidence—no spaceships, no alien bodies, no ray-guns. Second, if aliens had visited Earth, it would be such a huge event that it would certainly appear in historical records. Finally, if aliens had visited our planet, we would either continue to have contact with them or we would no longer exist because the aliens would have destroyed us in their attempt to take over our world. However, not only have extraterrestrials come to Earth, many live among us today. [CHALLENGE AN ESTABLISHED IDEA] All you need to do is take a look at the music recording industry to see that aliens like Elvis Presley, [BING!] Michael Jackson, [BOING!] and Mariah Carey [BANG!] surround us. [THESIS STATEMENT]

For starters, [TRANSITION] Elvis Presley must have been an alien. [BING!] Adult audiences were shocked when he swiveled his hips on stage, but this is merely the way in which his species walks. In addition, Elvis is known to have eaten peanut butter and banana sandwiches fried in butter almost daily. The chemical reaction that occurs when these ingredients are fried together creates a nutrient essential to alien life.

Lastly, many people work as Elvis impersonators. They are not cheap imitations, however. The look-a-likes simply belong to the same race of aliens as Elvis. As the first alien of his species to visit Earth, Elvis's job was to establish himself as a cultural icon, paving the way for thousands of extraterrestrials to find work in our society. [SUPPORTING SENTENCES]

A second alien who inhabits our planet [TRANSITION] is Michael Jackson. [BOING!] Although he claims that his face has changed over the years as a result of plastic surgery, the truth is that it has been slowly morphing back to its original alien shape. Further, Jackson made headlines when it was discovered that he sleeps in an oxygen chamber. The chamber actually fills with a gas that simulates the atmosphere of Jackson's home planet. Finally, Jackson uses phrases like hee-hee-hee and whoo-whoo-whoo in between his lyrics. Most people think these are just filler noises, but these sounds are words in Jackson's native language, which allow him to communicate with his fellow aliens here on Earth. [SUPPORTING SENTENCES]

Last, [TRANSITION] there is little doubt that Mariah Carey must be an alien. [BANG!] Very few human artists can reach notes as high as Carey or hold those notes nearly as long. The only reasonable explanation for this is that, like Michael Jackson, she communicates with other members of her species when she sings. However, Carey's voice is multilayered. Her native language is spoken at a high-pitched frequency that, when combined with her powerful voice, travels to her home planet in less than an hour. More proof that she is an alien can be found in her wardrobe. The skin-tight clothes that Carey wears are not made of any handmade materials but of a synthetic weave that forces her natural figure to assume a human shape. If she were to wear clothes made from materials found here on Earth, her body would loosen up and she would look more like the Michelin tire man. [SUPPORTING SENTENCES]

In conclusion, [TRANSITION] Elvis Presley, Michael Jackson, and Mariah Carey are merely the most obvious aliens to have danced and sung their ways into the hearts of humans. If one examines other artists, it quickly becomes clear that many more "people" should be classified as extraterrestrials. But why have so many aliens found work in the music industry? Perhaps the best explanation is that humans expect their singers to possess odd character quirks, to wear unusual clothing, and to have voices that cover several octaves. The music industry, therefore, provides aliens with the perfect cover. [MAKE THE READER THINK]

NOTE: The opinions expressed above are not necessarily those of the authors (or the publisher).

Yeah, sure. Whatever!

2. PROMPT—Do today's teen pop stars have any musical talent? (An argument essay)

Despite what many music critics say, today's teen pop stars do, in fact, have musical talent. [CHALLENGE AN ESTABLISHED IDEA] Britney Spears, the Backstreet Boys, and Mandy Moore did not simply wake up one morning and become pop stars. Each of these teen pop stars was born with three special talents that are shared by all of the legends of music: they can sing, [BING!] they can dance, [BOING!] and they can engage their audiences. [BANG!] Without these talents, they never would have been able to attract the attention of managers or record companies, much less the adoration of millions of young fans. [THESIS STATEMENT]

First, [TRANSITION] just about everyone knows how to sing, but unlike teen pop stars, most of us will never be able to do it well. [BING!] Singing lessons can add polish to a voice, but there is more to great singing than learning technical details. A great singer must accurately hit the high and low notes, and at the same time use his or her voice to share the emotions of a song with the audience. Combining these skills cannot be taught, so only those people who were born with truly exceptional voices have a chance of becoming successful entertainers. [SUPPORTING SENTENCES]

Second, [TRANSITION] the majority of teen pop stars are excellent dancers. [BOING!] Not every musician incorporates dance routines into his or her performances. But many serious and well-respected musicians, such as Peter Gabriel, Steven Tyler, and Madonna, do dance when they perform. To do it well, a person requires three skills: a sense of balance, the ability to move in time to music, and an ability to memorize intricate dance steps. These, too, are traits that not all people are born with. Yet teen pop stars kick, slide, and spin for two hours straight during concerts, and their videos feature them performing with backup dancers who have trained for years. They always land on their feet, they never miss a beat, and they rarely forget what they are supposed to do next. [SUPPORTING SENTENCES]

Last, [TRANSITION] every musical performer must be able to connect with his or her audience. [BANG!] This connection occurs as a result of the singer's ability to perform in such a way that the audience can feel the emotions of the song. Even if the singer is having a bad day, she must overcome it if she is performing a happy song. In a way, this is a lot like being able to act. And, like singing and dancing, it cannot be taught. Teen pop stars possess this talent as well. Without it, no matter how well they sing or dance, they would not attract large crowds of fans to their concerts or make anyone want to buy their albums. [SUPPORTING SENTENCES]

Every generation has had its own teen stars—David Cassidy and Donny Osmond in the 1970s, the New Kids on the Block in the 1980s, and Britney Spears, the Backstreet Boys, and Mandy Moore today. The critics have said that they were not musically talented. But if that were the case, these people would not have been so successful in their young careers. In fact, teen stars are gifted. They have managed to sing, dance, and engage their audiences well enough to sell millions of albums and concert tickets. [RESTATE THE THESIS] Therefore, we should not be so quick to call them untalented. [MAKE THE READER THINK]

3. PROMPT—Should pep rallies be an integral part of the high school experience? (An argument essay)

The gymnasium has been decorated in the school colors. Banners hang from the ceiling. The entire student population is herded onto the bleachers to cheer on their classmates who are about to take to the field or court against the school's archenemy. The marching band performs the school fight song as the names of the star athletes are announced over the PA system. Following a tradition that has existed at this school since the early 1920s, one athlete after another emerges from the locker room, wearing his team uniform and absorbing the energy from the crowd. [TAKE A PICTURE] Yet traditional pep rallies are an unfair activity to inflict upon today's high school students. [CHALLENGE AN ESTABLISHED IDEA] Rallies encourage segregation. [BING] They force students to be enthusiastic. [BOING] And they focus only on a narrow segment of the school's population. [BANG!] [THESIS STATEMENT]

To begin with, [TRANSITION] all year long, teachers and administrators attempt to instill values of equality and social justice in the minds and hearts of high school students. Yet the students who attend the rally are divided according to class and are encouraged to compete against one another to see whose class is "the best." [BING!] Seniors are given preferential treatment with the central-most group of bleachers, juniors and sophomores sit on their wings, and lowly freshmen are tucked away underneath the bleachers, out of sight and out of mind. It quickly becomes clear to all students present that diversity must be avoided at all costs and that, to be accepted by society, you must conform. [SUPPORTING SENTENCES]

Also, [TRANSITION] forcing teens to be enthusiastic about a school-related event rarely succeeds. [BOING!] Students who are not interested in the pep rally look at it instead as an opportunity to get out of class for a few periods. Further, at nearly every pep rally, there are always one or two students who go out of their way to disrupt the events by tormenting the freshmen and taunting the athletes with catcalls. When they "act up," the pep rally is halted and the entire school assembly is given a stern warning by the principal to behave themselves. As a result, the pep rally lasts longer, and the students who do not want to be there become even more easily distracted. [SUPPORTING SENTENCES]

Finally, [TRANSITION] while it is important to show your classmates that you support them in their extracurricular endeavors, the traditional pep rally does not address all students or all extracurricular activities. [BANG!] On the contrary, the vast majority of pep rallies are held in honor of athletes. Yet not all students engage in after-school sports. Some students prefer to exercise their minds with the choir or as Mathletes. Yet pep rallies for these students prior to competitions are nonexistent. [SUPPORTING SENTENCES]

In conclusion, [TRANSITION] the high school pep rally is a waste of a student's time. Students are encouraged to compete against one another in displays of "class pride." [BING!] They are forced to be enthusiastic, even though the majority of students have little interest in the pep rally. [BOING!] Finally, pep rallies celebrate the achievements of athletes while ignoring the achievements of other students. [BANG!] [RESTATEMENT OF THESIS] Until these drawbacks are resolved, pep rallies should not be permitted to take place in any high school. [MAKE THE READER THINK]

4. PROMPT—Who makes a better pet, a cat or a dog? (A compare/contrast essay)

You walk into your local animal shelter to adopt a pet. Dozens of adorable cats and dogs sit in cages and kennels, purring and barking. If you had your way, you would bring them all home. But then the voice of reason settles in and you decide to narrow down the choices to one. [TAKE A PICTURE] So, how do you pick just one when every animal is cute and cuddly? [ASK A QUESTION] The first thing you need to do is consider your lifestyle, because factors such as where you live, [BING!] how much time you spend at home, [BOING!] and how attached you want your pet to become to you [BANG!] will help you choose between a cat and a dog. [THESIS STATEMENT]

For starters, [TRANSITION] the size and location of your home can determine what kind of animal you adopt. [BING!] Cats, for example, adjust easily to any kind of home. Because they do not require a lot of space for exercise, they can live comfortably in either a small city apartment or on a large country estate. As long as there is access to a litter box and a few window ledges, a cat will be content in just about any kind of house. On the other hand, [TRANSITION] most dogs need plenty of room to run. They have boundless energy (especially when they are young) and need room to run around and play as they have a tendency to gain weight if they are not exercised often. Therefore, a studio apartment is not a good environment for a large dog like a Great Dane or a Saint Bernard, and it can be difficult to keep even a medium-sized dog, like a spaniel or a collie, in a city apartment. [SUPPORTING SENTENCES]

Another factor to consider [TRANSITION] is how much time you spend at home. [BOING!] If you work long hours or like to go away for long weekends, a cat makes for a great pet because it is an independent creature. Just leave out some fresh water and perhaps have a neighbor stop by to feed it each evening, and you can leave a cat home alone for several days or a full week without worry. Also, you only need to train a cat to do one thing: use its litter box. Once that skill has been mastered, a cat can be trusted not to get into trouble or be destructive when you are not with it. Dogs, however, [TRANSITION] cannot be left alone for more than 10 or 12 hours without having an "accident" on the rug or destroying a piece of furniture. Further, dogs must undergo extensive training. They need to be housebroken and taught how to walk on a leash and how to behave around guests. As a result, the time commitment to keeping a dog as a pet is immense, almost as great as having a child. And unlike a cat, you cannot leave it on its own for several days but must board it at a professional dog-care facility when you go on vacation. [SUPPORTING SENTENCES]

Last, [TRANSITION] you must look at the attachment factor. [BANG!] Domesticated cats are solitary animals that do not require a lot of attention. As kittens, they like to play with their owners, but once a cat matures, it prefers to be left alone. On occasion, it might come out of hiding to be petted or fed, but for the most part, a cat remains aloof. It will not eagerly await your return from work or school at the end of the day, nor will it come when you call it. In fact, the question most often asked in the home of a cat owner is "Have you seen the cat today?" On the other hand, [TRANSITION] a dog is a social creature that craves company and will do everything it can to get its owner to notice it. All you have to do is whistle or clap your hands, and your dog will come running to you. When you leave it alone in the house for a few hours, it will usually sit by the door and whimper until it hears your footsteps on the front porch. Then it will welcome you home by wagging its tail and licking your face. And once you are home, a dog will not let you out of its sight, following you everywhere you go. [SUPPORTING SENTENCES]

To conclude, [TRANSITION] when choosing between a cat and a dog as a pet, you must look at your lifestyle to determine which type of animal is better suited for you. Do you live in a small apartment? [BING!] Do you spend a lot of time away from home? [BOING!] And finally, do you cherish your privacy? [BANG!] If you answer yes to these questions, then a cat would be an appropriate pet. If, however, the opposite holds true, you should certainly consider getting a dog. [RESTATEMENT OF THESIS] Regardless of which type of animal you are better suited for, if you give your decision some thought first, you and your new pet will share a long, happy life together. [MAKE THE READER THINK]

5. PROMPT—If you could pick three people to live with in "The Real World" house, who would you pick and why?

What makes for a successful season of "The Real World?" [ASK A QUESTION] After having seen every episode at least three times, I believe that the most successful seasons are those in which the house includes people who are neat freaks, strategists, and peacemakers. Even though the whole point behind the show is that you do not get to decide who you live with, if I had a chance to pick my roommates, I would pick individuals who filled those three roles: Martha Stewart, [BING!] Napoleon Bonaparte, [BOING!] and Big Bird. [BANG!] [THESIS STATEMENT]

To begin with, [TRANSITION] whenever seven strangers live together, at least one will be a slob. For a while, the other roommates will yell at him to clean up his mess, but eventually they'll give up, get used to it, and become slobs, too. By the third or fourth week, the house will have hundreds of new residents—mice, roaches, and rats—and an exterminator will have to be called in. If, however, one of the roommates is a neat freak, she'll keep the house spotless. Martha Stewart is a perfect example of just such a person. [BING!] Through her magazine, television show, and books, she has shown millions of Americans how to clear up clutter through do-it-yourself projects. She weaves raffia into furniture, disguises toilet bowl brushes with sequins and bows, and turns empty soda cans into works of art. Thanks to Martha, not only would the house always look nice, the remaining roommates would never have to argue over who left the old pizza box under the sofa because either Martha would throw it out herself or she would use it for one of her craft projects. [SUPPORTING SENTENCES]

In addition, [TRANSITION] recent seasons have included episodes in which the casts of "The Real World" and "Road Rules" meet one another. For example, in the Miami season, one of the "Road Rules" missions was to steal the eight ball from "The Real World" pool table, and the second New York cast of "The Real World" faced off against the "Road Rules" team in a series of physical challenges. Through his ability to work out military campaigns, Napoleon Bonaparte was able to conquer most of Europe in fewer than ten years, rising to the position of Emperor. [BOING!] If a master of strategy like Napoleon lived in the house, no teams from any other MTV shows could even dream of defeating "The Real World" cast in the challenges. Another bonus to Napoleon living in the house: because he was so short, he could clean all the nooks and crannies that Martha Stewart is too tall to reach. [SUPPORTING SENTENCES]

Finally, [TRANSITION] with so many different kinds of people from such different backgrounds living together in a single house, arguments are bound to erupt over issues both big and small. People "stop being nice and start getting real" in "The Real World" house quickly, so I would choose a peacemaker as my third roommate. Big Bird's gentle voice and friendly personality make him one of the most loved characters on all of television. [BANG!] The majority of the people who live in "The Real World" house grew up watching his show, "Sesame Street," so chances are pretty good that they would listen to him when he stepped in to calm a tense situation. And if Big Bird could not reason with a roommate, all he would have to do is sit on that person. His feathers trap so much heat underneath his massive body that a couple of minutes underneath Big Bird would turn the most annoying, most unreasonable, and most difficult roommate into a perfect angel! [SUPPORTING SENTENCES]

By combining the talents of Martha Stewart, [BING!] Napoleon, [BOING!] and Big Bird, [BANG!] my version of "The Real World" house would be one of cleanliness, strength, and tranquility. [RESTATEMENT OF THESIS] Thanks to the personalities of these two people and one giant bird, all of the other roommates would naturally fall into line and get along for the four months that they would live together. There would be no disagreements and no feelings of inferiority to the casts of the other shows on the network. However, since this would not make for particularly exciting television, the likelihood of the executives at MTV actually agreeing to my choices is pretty remote. [MAKE THE READER THINK]

6. PROMPT—Defend or refute the following statement from the film *Forrest Gump:* "Life is like a
box of chocolates—you never know what you're
going to get."

The saying, "Life is like a box of chocolates—you
never know what you're going to get" currently holds
true. Most of the time, we can only guess at what
will happen in the future. However, scientists in the
fields of statistics, [BING!] meteorology, [BOING!]
and genetics [BANG!] are constantly collecting data
and making new discoveries that eliminate some of
the surprises of life. We will never be able to predict
the future with absolute certainty, but we will be able
to come close. [THESIS STATEMENT] [MAKE A
PREDICTION]

First, [TRANSITION] there is the science of
statistics. [BING!] Statisticians collect information
about regularly occurring events and use mathematical
formulas to predict how those events will turn out in
the future. With statistics, we can reasonably
determine the likelihood of hitting it rich on the
lottery or which horse will win first place at the
Kentucky Derby. However, statistics is, as yet, not
an exact science. Even though your favorite hockey
team is predicted to be the odds-on-favorite to win
the championship this year, there is always a chance
that the team could lose. The team's top scorer might

break his leg or sit out half the game in the penalty box. [SUPPORTING SENTENCES] Unexpected events can still turn predictions upside-down, but statistics can reasonably narrow the odds.

Another example [TRANSITION] of how we try to predict the future is meteorology. [BOING!] Like statisticians, meteorologists collect information about previous weather events. Then they compare current conditions to those of the past and forecast what the weather will be in the future. As a result, we can be fairly certain if it will rain on the Fourth of July parade or if we will have a "white" Christmas. But, also like statistics, meteorology is not an exact science. Every now and then, the weather forecaster predicts clear skies, but out of nowhere, a tornado touches down. Or you hear on the radio that a light dusting of snow will fall during the night, but when you wake up the next morning, there is a three-foot drift in your driveway. [SUPPORTING SENTENCES] All it takes is for the wind to unexpectedly change direction, and the usually precise forecast goes out the window.

A third science [TRANSITION] that helps us to predict the future is genetics. [BANG!] By studying the genetic codes that create life, scientists have been able to isolate the genes that define who we are. They are now learning how to predict whether a child will have blue eyes, grow up to be 6-feet tall, or be allergic to tree pollen before he or she is born. Although the technology does not yet exist, down the road scientists will be able to manipulate those codes. This will be a useful tool to prevent hereditary diseases, but there is also a risk that parents will ask their doctors to create "designer" babies—children who are genetically altered before birth to be smarter or prettier than they would have been without the alteration. [SUPPORTING SENTENCES] Regardless of the ethical issues, genetics, unlike statistics and meteorology, has a more promising future of allowing us to make accurate predictions.

In conclusion, [TRANSITION] the statement "life is like a box of chocolates—you never know what you're going to get" holds true today. However, the more data that statisticians and scientists like meteorologists and geneticists collect, the less true that statement becomes. Life will never become completely predictable. Unexpected surprises will always pop up. But eventually unpredictability will become the exception, not the rule. [MAKE THE READER THINK]

---

7. PROMPT—Write an essay in which you compare or contrast the heroes from your two most-favorite action/adventure films.

On the surface, Han Solo and Indiana Jones seem to be very different characters. One is a space smuggler who is only interested in getting rich. The other is a college professor who finds archaeological treasures for museums. But do these characters share any qualities? [ASK A QUESTION] Surprisingly, the answer is yes. [CHALLENGE AN ESTABLISHED IDEA] When you look closely at Solo and Jones, three major similarities come to light. Each is fearless, ingenious, and willing to risk his life to save the lives of others. [THESIS STATEMENT] As a result, they are much more alike than most people realize.

The first trait [TRANSITION] that Han Solo and Indiana Jones share is fearlessness. [BING!] For example, to escape Imperial cruisers in The Empire Strikes Back, Han pilots his ship into an asteroid field, even though the odds of success are "approximately 3,720 to 1." Han is confident, however, that his plan will work because he believes his pursuers would "be crazy to follow." Similarly, [TRANSITION] Indiana risks his life in Temple of Doom when he is trapped on a rope bridge. Rather than risk capture, he cuts the bridge in half with his machete. The soldiers who are pursuing him fall into the ravine below, where they are eaten by

---

hungry crocodiles, while Indiana dangles against the side of a cliff, the cut rope wrapped around his leg. [SUPPORTING SENTENCES] Both characters face danger fearlessly, perhaps even recklessly, yet their daring actions always result in success.

A second trait[TRANSITION] shared by Solo and Jones is the ability to quickly get out of tight spots. (BOING!) While hiding in the asteroid field, Solo devises a brilliant plan to avoid capture: He flies his Millennium Falcon straight toward an Imperial cruiser. But at the last second, rather than crash into the cruiser, he lands on its roof. The Imperial troops can no longer detect the Falcon on their radar, so they mistakenly believe that Solo has escaped. Likewise, [TRANSITION] Jones finds fast solutions to dangerous situations. To escape a pilotless airplane in Temple of Doom, he grabs an emergency raft and, with Willie and Short Round clutching his back, jumps out the door. First, they land on a snow-covered mountain, where they ride the raft like a sled. Then they fly off a cliff and into a raging river, where they stay safely afloat until they can put in to shore. [SUPPORTING SENTENCES] As a result of their creative solutions, Solo and Jones easily elude capture and death.

The final trait [TRANSITION] shared by both characters is a willingness to risk their lives to save others. [BANG!] At first, Han refuses to help the

Rebel Alliance in Star Wars. "Attacking that battle station ain't my idea of courage. It's more like suicide," he declares. However, just as the Death Star is about to destroy the Rebel base and as Darth Vadar is about to fire on Luke's spaceship, Han comes to the rescue, saving both his friend's life and the Alliance. In the same way, [TRANSITION] Indiana puts his own life at risk to save his father, Henry, in The Last Crusade. Henry is shot in the stomach and can only be cured by water poured from the Holy Grail. However, the Grail lies beyond "three devices of lethal cunning"— saw blades that fly out of walls, a pit of spikes, and a wide canyon. One false step, and Indiana will die, but he thinks only of his father as he conquers each obstacle.[SUPPORTING SENTENCES] Han and Indiana never hesitate to come to the rescue of the people they care about, even if it means putting their own lives at risk.

At first glance,[TRANSITION] Han Solo and Indiana Jones seem to be very different people. Yet, when they are placed side by side, they turn out to share personality traits that are greatly admired: fearlessness, ingenuity, and self-sacrifice. [RESTATE THESIS IN NEW WAY] It is little wonder that they have been admired by movie audiences for nearly thirty years. [MAKE THE READER THINK]

A Word About Creative Writing

Once Upon a Time . . . Where do you go in your mind when you hear those words? Perhaps you're lying in bed under warm covers (you're maybe five, six years old?) and your mom or dad is reading to you right before your bedtime. You're feeling kind of drowsy, but the words are keeping you kind of awake as you start imagining the knights in shining armor prancing with their steeds across golden wheat fields . . . Or maybe you are listening to tales of fairies, elves, and goblins in enchanted lands where magic spells are potent and stronger than any monster you could possibly need to defy.

205

www.petersons.com   *Get Wise! Mastering Writing Skills*

Once Upon a Time may mean different things to different people, but for many of us it means that a page is turned and a whole new world of colorful characters, places and events have opened up before our eyes. It marks the beginning of a story. And a story is quite different from an essay.

While most of this book has focused on how to write an essay, we have also taught you (at least we hope!) a bit about how to get your brain stimulated enough to start thinking about different ideas and to write down how you feel about things. In addition, we talked about how to put words and sentences together so that you can express yourself clearly and in a way that is interesting to the reader. We're hoping that you had a little fun, and we're also hoping that you *really* enjoyed yourself and want to write more than just essays. You certainly can use a lot of the things we taught you here to get started, but a really smart, or *wise*, way to become a writer is to start writing down your thoughts every day. And guess what? You don't have to worry about topic sentences, thesis statements, or any of that. In fact, you don't have to even think about it making sense. Just write for yourself! As we said earlier, the more practice you get, the easier the words will come and suddenly you'll find it is as natural as breathing!

Some of you might want to start a journal. You can even call it "Once Upon a Time" and look at it as your own private world that you are creating with your own characters, your own places, and your own thoughts. You could show it to someone: like a parent, teacher, or friend—or not.

Think about reading this, say, 10 years from now! Imagine how you, 10 years older, will feel seeing the world from your younger self's eyes? Perhaps you have a story of time travel to tell? The point is you can do anything you'd like in this journal, and we promise it will bring you closer to that dream of being a writer one day.

Well, we have finally come to the end of this little book, and we're glad we were able to end it on this kind of positive note. Can you believe this journey is over?

Wait one minute! We are NOT going to get all weepy or anything over this. I didn't say *anything* **about that once upon a time stuff, and you have to know how tough** *that* **was! Repeat after me now: Goodbye, goodnight, ta-ta, adios, see ya!...**

Well then, okay. Goodbye dear reader. Keep writing, and good luck!

Later!

Notes

Notes

Notes